Jaclyn

Be a vessel for honor —

2 Timothy 2:20, 21

The Master's Work

Marilyn F. McClurg

The Master's Work

Marilyn F. McClurg

THE MASTER'S WORK
By: Marilyn F. McClurg
Copyright © 2011
GOSPEL FOLIO PRESS
All Rights Reserved

Published by
GOSPEL FOLIO PRESS
304 Killaly St. W.
Port Colborne, ON L3K 6A6
CANADA

ISBN: 9781926765488

Cover design by Danielle Elzinga

All Scripture quotations, unless otherwise indicated, are taken from the New King James Version ®. Copyright © 1982 by Thomas Nelson, Inc. Used by permission. All rights reserved.

Scripture quotations noted KJV are from The Hebrew-Greek Key Word Study Bible King James Version, © 1984, 1991, by AMG Publishers.

Printed in USA

This book is dedicated

in abiding affection

to my "sister-by-prayer."

Contents

1. That You May Marvel 9
2. Small And Common 17
3. Safely Home 27
4. Divine Purpose 35
5. Ownership Established 47
6. Under Construction 57
7. Grace And Glory 67
8. Sovereignty 75
9. Precious Promises 85
10. Omnipotence 95
Appendix 105
Endnotes 109
Scripture Index 113

1. That You May Marvel

What does it take to make you marvel? In a society gone mad with desire for loud entertainment, interest in outlandish celebrities, and preoccupation with electronic gimmickry, when do you make time to listen to God speak? Where do you look to see the Master at work? What quiets your heart and satisfies your soul? The psalmists readily acknowledged God's all-pervasive presence and took delight in praising Him for His marvelous works, His marvelous kindness, and His marvelous wonders.

Customarily Jewish pilgrims, as they climbed the hill to Jerusalem on their way to religious observance, sang the praise psalms together in preparation for worship. One of these songs, Psalm 118, includes a most amazing prophecy concerning the coming Messiah:

> *"The stone which the builders rejected*
> *Has become the chief cornerstone.*
> *This was the* LORD*'s doing;*
> *It is marvelous in our eyes"* (Ps. 118:22, 23).

Those early pilgrims did not understand the implication of the words they sang together; nevertheless, they joyously acknowledged God's sovereign authority at work and they marveled.

Like the psalmists, who sang of God's marvelous works, the four Gospel writers record specific times when men marveled at the works of the Lord Jesus Christ. Matthew describes a great tempest that caused the disciples to fear they might perish. Despite their unbelief, Jesus calmed the wind and the sea, and *"the men marveled"* (Matt. 8:27). Mark writes of the man possessed by a legion of demons that Jesus set free. He went about all Decapolis proclaiming what *"Jesus had done for him; and all marveled"* (Mark 5:20). Witnesses to these supernatural events decided for themselves that these **works** merited wonder.

In much the same way, they determined if and when **words** of wisdom merited their acclaim. Luke explains how Jesus Christ handled the question posed by the chief priests and the scribes: *"Is it lawful for us to pay taxes to Caesar or not?"* The Savior knowing their *"craftiness,"* asked whose image appeared on a Roman coin. They answered, *"Caesar's."* He said to them, *"'Render therefore to Caesar the things that are Caesar's and to God the things that are God's'... And they marveled at His answer"* (Luke 20:22-26). John records how Jesus went up to the temple during the Feast of Tabernacles and taught, to the amazement of those who heard His words. *"'How does this Man know letters, having never studied?' And the Jews marveled"* (John 7:14, 15). These demonstrations of Jesus' authority, wisdom, and spiritual perception produced a similar response in all who witnessed these events: they stopped to marvel; they expressed astonishment.

In addition to the many signs and wonders recorded in his gospel account, John focuses a spotlight on the reasons Jesus Himself gave for His words: *"As My Father taught Me, I speak these things"* (8:28). *"I speak what I have seen with My Father"* (8:38). *"I have not spoken on my own authority; but the Father who sent Me gave Me a command, what I should say and what I should speak. And I know that His command is everlasting life. Therefore, what ever I speak, just as the Father has told Me, so I speak"* (12:49, 50). Jesus' words and works are inextricably bound up with the Father because they are His words and works: He authorized them, and they testify to the eternal oneness of the Son with the Father.

John focuses attention on one of these works, an event that took place in Jerusalem one Sabbath day during a feast of the Jews, an occasion which Christ used to teach His disciples when it is appropriate to marvel and when it is not. A man, who had been lame thirty-eight years, lay helplessly among the great multitude of sick people waiting and hoping to be healed at the Pool of Bethesda. Jesus singled him out and asked if he wanted to be made whole. When the man answered that he had no one to lower him in the pool, Jesus told him, *"'Rise, take up your bed and walk.' And immediately the man was made well, took up his bed and walked"* (John 5:8, 9). The unbelieving Jews considered this miracle a trespass against the law which forbade work on the Sabbath and were so furious with the Lord Jesus that they sought to kill Him. But Christ took this opportunity to explain how the Father and Son, together, work their sovereign purpose:

> *"Most assuredly, I say to you, the Son can do nothing of Himself, but what He sees the Father do; for whatever He does, the Son also does in like manner. For the Father loves the Son, and shows Him all things that He Himself does; and He will show Him greater works than these, that you may marvel"* (John 5:19, 20).

Jesus went on to explain to this angry crowd that the Father had given Him the power of eternal life: *"Most assuredly, I say to you, the hour is coming, and now is, when the dead will hear the voice of the Son of God; and those who hear will live"* (John 5:25). Then He warned them: *"Do not marvel at this; for the hour is coming in which all who are in the graves will hear [My] voice and come forth"* (John 5:28, 29). They were **not** to marvel at the supernatural work of resurrection from the dead. They **were** to marvel at the interactive work of the Father and the Son.

Jesus' works so amazed Nicodemus, a ruler of the Jews, that he came under the cover of darkness to hear the words of the young Rabbi who told him that unless he believed that he needed a new birth he could not see the kingdom of God. This strange teaching astonished Nicodemus, and he protested his ignorance. Jesus gently chided him with these words, *"Do not marvel that I said to you, 'You must be born again'"* (John 3:7). The Savior's words were plain and precise: if the ruler of the Jews expected to see the kingdom of God, a new birth was necessary. But Nicodemus was **not** to marvel at the supernatural work that takes place when one is born again. Christ Jesus, our Lord, the final authority about how we are to think about supernatural events, says we are **not** to marvel. In marked contrast, we learn from Jesus' explanation of the interaction within the Godhead that the marvelous way the Son has declared the Father is intended to elicit wonder. The words and works of the Father, Son, and Holy Spirit should cause us to marvel!

The psalmists got it right: time and again they direct our attention to the marvelous works of the Creator and His marvelous kindness. Elihu got it right when he proclaimed the majesty of God's voice, *"God thunders marvelously with His voice; He does great things which we cannot comprehend"* (Job 37:5). Micah got it right when he declared the marvelous things God showed to His people when He brought them out of the land of Egypt (Mic. 7:15). Yes, the psalmists marvel at the work of God, and the prophets speak forth more wonders. Through their mouths, God announced to the entire world His intentions: *"Look among the nations and watch—Be utterly astounded! For I will work a work in your days which you would not believe, though it were told you"* (Hab. 1:5).

> *"Therefore, behold,*
> *I will again do a marvelous work among the people,*
> *A marvelous work and a wonder"* (Isa. 29:14).

This astonishing future work to which God refers is the redemptive sacrifice of His own Son, accomplished at Calvary in fulfillment of the Father's eternal plan to redeem men. Jesus Christ defined this work in a series of statements: *"My Father has been working until now, and I have been working"* (John 5:17). *"This is the work of God, that you believe in Him whom He sent"* (John 6:29). *"I must work the works of Him who sent Me while it is day; the night is coming when no one can work"* (John 9:4). *"I told you, and you do not believe. The works that I do in My Father's name, they bear witness of Me"* (John 10:25). *"I have glorified* [Him] *on the earth. I have finished the work which* [He gave] *Me to do"* (John 17:4). And when, from that cross of suffering and shame, He cried out to His Father, *"It is finished,"* He proclaimed to all people, and for all time, that the marvelous work of redemption was complete. Without controversy, those who believe should never cease to marvel.

God desires us to marvel when, in perfect harmony, the Father and Son work to reveal their sovereign purpose. But there is more, for Jesus said, *"The Helper, the Holy Spirit, whom the Father will send in My name, He will teach you all things, and bring to your remembrance all things that I said to you... And when He has come, He will convict the world of sin, and of righteousness, and of judgment"* (John 14:26; 16:8). The work of redemption is complete, but since the day of Pentecost, the Father, Son, and Holy Spirit continue to work together drawing men to believe. When we see the outworking of this wondrous love we should marvel. Writing to new believers, Paul expands this idea of wonderment as he unfolds the wisdom of God:

> *"As it is written:*
> *'Eye has not seen, nor ear heard,*
> *Nor have entered into the heart of man*
> *The things which God has prepared for those who love Him.'*
> *But God has revealed them to us through His Spirit"* (1 Cor. 2:9, 10).

God's eternal plan for each of us, and the outworking of that plan, are inherently amazing and wondrous, and believers ought to observe and marvel as He unfolds His perfect will.

What can we say of unbelievers concerning this matter? In my youth, I was cynical, self-centered, prone to anger, and rebellious, as Judah and Jerusalem, and needed correction. God's description of Israel could have been said of me:

> *"I have nourished and brought up children,*
> *And they have rebelled against Me;*
> *The ox knows its owner and the donkey its master's crib;*

The Master's Work

But Israel does not know,
My people do not consider" (Isa. 1:2, 3).

I did not know my Master. I did not consider God. But, like many unbelievers, I responded to that which stirred my emotions, or produced admiring surprise, or amazement.

My earliest recollection of the marvelous occurred as Mother read aloud the story of a young girl, much like me, who needed a great transformation. *The Good Master* is the story of Kate, a city girl, who comes by train from Budapest to live with her uncle's family on their large ranch. Kate's father, in a letter to his brother Marton, describes her as a "most impossible, incredible, disobedient, headstrong little imp" and he pleads with Marton, "Try to put a halter on my wild colt."[1] Ten year old Jancsi, disciplined, patient, and warm-hearted, is totally unprepared for his utterly unpredictable cousin Kate. A picturesque account of daily farm life on the Hungarian plain follows. The reader comes to see why Uncle Marton, loved by farm hands and ranchers alike, is considered the "good master," for he is wise, kind, and persevering. Slowly and steadily in the months that follow, Kate is irresistibly won over as she yields herself to his authority and responds to his love. The marvelous transformation is real and complete.

As a child, I was much like Kate: untamed, wild, and hiding my desire for some small measure of improvement. This enchanting story provided me with a glimpse of what a good master should be and what he could enable if only one would allow it. A seed of hope had been sown in my soul, but many years of frustration lay ahead before I came to meet my Good Master, the Lord Jesus Christ. Like Nicodemus, I was slow in recognizing my need of a Saviour, slow to believe, and equally slow to marvel at His patient and persistent work in my life.

Countless writers have investigated the unique character of the marvelous work of God as He draws men to Himself. George MacDonald, the nineteenth century Scottish writer, explores the Master's shaping work in a collection of sonnets

That You May Marvel

published in 1880, under the title, *A Book of Strife*, now available as 366 devotionals in the *Diary of An Old Soul*. In the same way that Isaiah, Paul, and Peter likened their earthly life to a tent (See Appendix, Note A), MacDonald refers to himself as a "homeless wanderer," and laments his "fluttering tent." He cries to God, "fill [my] tent with laughing morn's delight," and explores the way the Master works with common things. He goes on to say that our necessary response "is to heed humbly every smallest thing," thus permitting God to "turn all our old things to new."[2] In the stanzas that follow, MacDonald unfolds the marvelous process by which the Master designs and builds a spiritual house for His own royal majesty, and thus the poet sees his own prayer answered.

From MacDonald's sixteen sonnets, that define the supernatural drawing and transforming work of God, I have selected three stanzas to set the stage and provide the organization for our exploration of *The Master's Work*.

> Well mayst Thou then work on indocile hearts
> By small successes, disappointment small;
> By nature, weather, failure, or sore fall;
> By shame, anxiety, bitterness, and smarts;
> By loneliness, by weary loss of zest:
> The rags, the husks, the swine, the hunger-quest,
> Drive home the wanderer to the Father's breast!

> Too eager I must not be to understand.
> How should the work the Master goes about
> Fit the vague sketch my compasses have planned?
> I am His house—for Him to go in and out.
> He builds me now—and if I cannot see
> At any time what He is doing with me,
> 'Tis that He makes the house for me too grand.

The Master's Work

> The house is not for me—it is for Him.
> His royal thoughts require many a stair,
> Many a tower, many an outlook fair,
> Of which I have no thought, and need no care.
> Where I am most perplexed, it may be there
> Thou mak'st a secret chamber, holy-dim,
> Where Thou wilt come to help my deepest prayer.[3]

Come with me as we explore the Master's work and consider some of the marvelous ways He draws people to Himself, and "turns our old things to new," that we may marvel.

2. Small And Common

> Well mayst Thou then work on indocile hearts
> By small successes, disappointments small;
> By nature, weather, failure, or sore fall;
> By shame, anxiety, bitterness, and smarts; —GMD

Luke, the beloved physician, author of the Acts of the Apostles, records many small and common details about the life of Saul, who is also called Paul (Acts 13:9). The apostle labeled himself the chief of sinners, and records, for our benefit, the reason for God's mercy in his own life: *"That in me first Jesus Christ might show all longsuffering, as a pattern to those who are going to believe on Him for everlasting life"* (1 Tim. 1:16). As I reflect upon the Master's patient and persistent work on my own sinful heart, I observe a similar pattern emerging from the shadows of my childhood. Even though rebellion had not yet sprouted, the seeds lay dormant, as if waiting for any storm that might precipitate a crisis.

George MacDonald's use of the word "indocile" is an accurate description of my teenage years. My heart was unruly, noncompliant, obstinate, ungovernable, and too wild to recognize the abject slavery that results from such behaviour. I was indeed not easy to teach or discipline, although a variety of long-suffering instructors applied themselves to my training.

Mother taught me to type, and I found great pleasure in perfectly aligned columns of words and phrases. When she decided that I had properly learned touch typing, she began sewing lessons, and I discovered the satisfaction that comes with cutting pieces of fabric apart and putting them back together. We made aprons, simple skirts and blouses; later came tailoring procedures, and then how to design and create beautiful hand-pieced quilts.

The Master's Work

Mother was wonderfully creative in a variety of ways. A gifted storyteller, she truly loved books and considered them treasure boxes to be opened in expectation, with clean hands and a ready mind. Brother and I caught her fascination with the written word, both poetry and prose. Lewis Carroll and A. A. Milne staked claim in my heart, and many of the poems I learned in my elementary school years I can still recite fairly accurately. Their familiar meters never fail to revive pleasant memories of Mother brushing and coaxing my long hair into thick braids as we repeated lines of poetry together. She read to us all the time, and eventually began a weekly "reading hour" for neighbour kids who came and sat cross-legged in a circle on the floor. She introduced them to good literature and taught them how to use the local library.

Almost every Saturday Mother baked sweet yeast breads. The delicious aroma filled the house with a fragrance that lasted for hours, a lingering evidence of her love for us. Monday was always wash day. I loved the gleaming copper washtub and the smell of soapy water and steaming clothes. After the labour of washing, came the sheer joy of being outdoors and the challenge of hanging laundry on a clothesline I could barely reach. Mother taught me how to stretch the sheets taut, how to match up socks in pairs, and how to arrange colors like a rainbow. Together we rejoiced when everything danced in the wind. Some simple pleasures we never outgrow, and I still experience a deep sense of satisfaction in the feel of old hardcover books, the rich scent of yeast dough baking, and the sight of clothes floating in the breeze. These things never fail to lift my heart in thanksgiving.

Mother taught us a deep respect for authority, but obedience was not easy for I was willful and determined. My fourth-grade room on an outside corner of the school building provided windows in two directions. I spent a great deal of time watching the shadows play on the piled snow banks. One such ordinary morning, my reverie was interrupted when my teacher instructed me to report to the principal's office. Fear gripped my heart. As far as I knew, an order to the principal's office was the worst possible thing that could happen to a student. With a heavy sense of dread, I dragged myself from the room and proceeded very slowly down that dark, terribly long hallway to the main office, entered, and was told to sit and wait. I had plenty of time to regret my flash of anger that morning when I had thoughtlessly thrown a snowball at another student. I knew snowballs were strictly forbidden and felt overwhelmed by guilt.

I suffered in black despair as I waited to hear my punishment. Instead, the principal welcomed me into her office. With an encouraging smile, she informed me that a book review I had submitted had won national acclaim in a contest sponsored by the New York Times. I could hardly believe my ears. I was expecting punishment, but no, I had been summoned for reward! I need not take home a report of my angry act of disobedience. But, what should have been a time of joy and satisfaction was sullied by guilt. I marvel to think that God planned this special lesson because I needed correction. My guilt and shame reduced this honour to a "small success" as God used it to warn me of my propensity to disobey. God judged and put me down, thus preventing any inclination to feel superior. Sincerely ashamed, I found no pleasure in the award or the public ceremony that followed.

Although God was not in my thoughts at this time, He was at work on my unruly heart. For reasons I cannot recall, I asked and then argued, for permission to visit a different Sunday school than the one I frequently attended near our home. With parental consent, I set off on the long walk by myself. The Sunday school teacher made a profound impression that is still bearing fruit in my life. I have no recollection of her name, her appearance, or what she taught, but for the first time in my experience, I met someone who knew that she had been forgiven. I marveled at her serenity and the bold confidence she had in God. I had no idea how that forgiveness had been achieved, but she was so certain of her God that even this obstinate eight-year-old could see that confidence. I wanted that forgiveness for myself and waited expectantly for each class. But, the fourth weekend it rained, and then it poured. Walking was out of the question, and I wept bitterly. The next week, Mother refused to allow me to go, and I never saw her again. I did know that my heart was not right in the sight of God (Acts 8:21), but I did not know that He was already preparing the ground of my heart for His seed, the Word of God. In His own mysterious way, the Master, worked through this faithful Sunday school teacher who radiated the peace that follows forgiveness.

The following summer I enjoyed the distinct privilege of participating in a French class at the local university. Only nine years old, I rode the streetcar by myself, mingled with college students on campus, and spoke only French for three hours every morning all summer. The department head decided to reward the class for hard work: we would demonstrate our mastery of the language through a presentation of "Cinderella." We had tryouts and then endless rehearsals. I managed a small role as one of the cruel step-sisters. A whole new world opened for me: the bright lights, the huge, heavy curtain, elegant costumes, make-up, learning stage entries and exits, and the strange idea of a prompter—each one a new challenge, and I was delirious with excitement. Dress rehearsal seemed perfect. Cinderella seemed perfect. I seemed perfect. Surely I was destined for the stage!

The performance before parents and friends proved a great success. No one forgot his or her lines or tripped on the props. The Prince found the one whose foot fit the glass slipper, and the audience applauded right on cue. But all the sparkle had disappeared for me. The thrill and excitement lay in the planning and preparation, not in the final presentation. A "disappointment small," but I immediately abandoned my plans for a career on the stage; no name in lights for me, and I felt no regret.

Winning a coveted award had brought no joy because of my sense of guilt; now my pride on stage resulted in boredom rather than pleasure. I did not know that God was at work, but David understood when he wrote these words:

> "For exaltation comes neither from the east
> Nor from the west nor from the south.
> But God is the Judge:
> He puts down one,
> And exalts another" (Ps. 75:6, 7).

Small and Common

God had judged and put me down, permitting no exaltation, but His tender care was evident as both success and disappointment were kept "small."

We see in MacDonald's sonnets how frequently he expresses his deeply felt need for God's continual work in his soul. In a similar fashion, Charles Wesley describes his early years of sin and unbelief in two unforgettable lines: "Long my imprisoned spirit lay, Fast bound in sin and Nature's night."[1] Like Wesley, we lament the lingering effects of sin's corrupting presence. The apostle Paul included us when he spoke of the *"sons of disobedience, among whom also we all once conducted ourselves... fulfilling the desires of the flesh and of the mind, and were by nature children of wrath"* (Eph. 2:2, 3). Indeed, each of us stands guilty before God, but He, the great and faithful Master, works on our very nature, and I can testify to you, *"The Lord is not slack concerning His promise... but is longsuffering toward us, not willing that any should perish but that all should come to repentance"* (2 Pet. 3:9). Yes. God gave His promise, provided for my redemption, and quietly continues His work on my obstinate heart. He used the small and common events of daily life. He used success, disappointment, and failure to bring me to a place where ultimately I would hear the Master's voice and respond to His work in my life.

In his poem, MacDonald named a variety of things God uses to accomplish His shaping work in stubborn hearts. He lists: weather, sore fall, shame, anxiety, bitterness, and smarts. I read this list, and wonder how he could have foreseen the path of learning the Master planned for me.

In northern Ohio where I grew up, the seasonal weather changes provide a reliable memory aid; many small and common events in my childhood can be associated with the weather. Dry flakes of snow blew in swirls about the car as our family made the long drive from Cleveland to Detroit in the December cold. I was ten and a half years old. The year was 1941. Weeks earlier, we had received word that my nineteen year old cousin had died very suddenly. Despite my parents' obvious grief, there was no mention of going to the funeral. Now, however, we were going to pay our belated respects and try to be some measure of comfort to our relatives. Uncertain of the meaning of the word "consolation," I sensed nevertheless that we were undertaking a sober thing, and the blowing snow punctuated my thoughts. Upon our arrival, we found my aunt and uncle in deep mourning. My cousin lowered her voice whenever she referred to her departed younger brother. The silences seemed awkward, and, finally when the somber evening came to a close, we went to our beds.

The next morning we all sat uncomfortably on straight-backed chairs in the living room. The conversation held no interest for me, and I sat there wishing we could get started for home. When someone turned on the radio, we heard the solemn voice of President Roosevelt announcing, "Japan has bombed Pearl Harbor! We are at war. This day shall live in infamy." I had no idea what any of these words meant, but the face of every adult in the room told the story. There could be no misunderstanding that "war" and "infamy" must surely be horrible beyond description. In the stunned silence that followed, someone remarked that Aunt and Uncle should be thankful that their son would not face the inevitable horror of fighting a war in some foreign land. These words seemed to bring a good measure of comfort to the adults in the room, and shortly thereafter we got into our car and left.

I had hours to consider this strange comfort on the long drive home. I could not understand the sudden change in the adults. How could death seem so awful and then suddenly seem to be okay just because war caused more death? I came to the conclusion that it must be the nature of war that every young man called to fight would surely die in battle; therefore, my cousin had escaped a greater tragedy. Mother could well have explained away my confusion, but she and Father were unusually quiet, so I refrained from voicing my questions and retreated in silence. Choosing to entertain these dark and fearful thoughts was like digging myself into a deep ditch. We often do just that when we think we understand something that we cannot begin to comprehend. The psalmist correctly describes the folly of my black mood and its inevitable results:

Small and Common

"Behold, the wicked...
Conceives trouble and brings forth falsehood.
He made a pit and dug it out,
And has fallen into the ditch which he made" (Ps. 7:14, 15).

I fell into the ditch of my own making, and God used my "failure" and "sore fall" as He continued to work on my immature heart.

Mother, the consummate teacher, enjoyed telling stories about our relatives and always included many small and common details. My favorite family history concerned my paternal great-grandparents who experienced a different kind of fall themselves. Although they already had four daughters, they adopted another girl. Grandmother and her sisters were brought up to do fancy sewing and such things as people of the privileged class did. Great-grandfather's draying business provided so well for the family that my grandmother had her own pony and cart when she attended private school in Canada, and as a young woman, she spent some time in Paris. The draying business was already declining in the early 1880's when the West Third Street Bridge in Cleveland collapsed. Two of Great-grandfather's workmen, together with their teams and wagons, went down with the bridge. Great-grandfather voluntarily took on the support of both those families, and from that day forward, his own family was reduced to very ordinary circumstances. I thought long and hard about his commitment to care for those individuals as if they were his kin, and came to admire his moral purpose. Childlike, I wondered what made him so willing to sacrifice his own wealth and felt quite proud that I had such a noble great-grandfather. Every time Mother told this story, I would resolve to imitate him, to do always what seemed to me to be right. I saw each fresh resolve as a small success, but I was helpless to change my behaviour, and my prideful heart was set for another fall.

In addition to storytelling, Mother taught me to enjoy kitchen duties. By the time I was eleven, she entrusted the entire after-supper cleanup to me. The day had been very hot, but the windows were wide open to the cool evening breeze and the sound of buzzing insects. While I was drying the supper dishes, my brother ventured outside to explore and somehow put himself in the path of a moving automobile. A neighbour came to the door shouting for my Father, who was in the bathtub. In what seemed but a few seconds, Father emerged completely dressed. I watched in amazement as he ran off in his socks, carrying his shoes while Mother and I stood helpless. Slowly, a group of neighbours gathered in our living room to offer well-intentioned assurances that all would be well. It seemed a very long while before Father returned. I saw that he had his shoes on and that he looked very tired. My limping brother's head was wound up in bandages. Mother burst into tears. The neighbours all began to talk at the same time as they gathered around "the poor little lamb." I stood alone, jealous of all the attention my brother was getting and wondering if they would have made such a fuss if I had been the one hit by a car. Just as quickly as the jealousy had reared its ugly head, came jealousy's reward: an appalling sense of shame, so forceful as to make me sick to my stomach. I saw myself as truly sinful and very wicked. *"Shame covered my face... I became a stranger to my brother"* (Ps. 69:7, 8). I felt so isolated by my own sense of guilt that I never told my brother how glad I was that his injuries were not worse. However, my shame didn't change me much; so it was but another "small success."

I failed to comfort my aunt and uncle as I had wanted to do. I failed to live up to the moral standard of my Great-grandfather. And, I failed miserably when I did not respond to my brother's accident in a way that I knew was right. God was using these failures to move me, but something far more critical was about to happen that He would use to shape my soul.

I became more self-absorbed the year following my brother's accident, focusing all my energy on my school work and my grades. I was aware that Mother's teaching efforts had ceased and that she never read to us any more, but I was too self-centered to notice her failing health. She went to the hospital to have a goiter removed and returned home with a frighteningly ugly red scar across her lovely, white throat. The doctor said it would fade, but I studied it closely every day, and he was wrong. Mother's continuing physical ailments began to blend with emotional instability until at last her overstressed nervous system broke down. I well remember the beautiful spring day when life as I knew it came to an end. Oblivious to the seriousness of Mother's deteriorating emotional state, I had been planning for my thirteenth birthday. The air was filled with the songs of birds and heavy with the scent of lily-of-the-valley when total strangers came and forcefully carried Mother off to a mental institution. My childhood came to a grinding halt.

I longed to know what had happened to my mother, but everyone responded to my questions by saying that I was too young to understand. My anxiety and frustration turned to bitterness, and I resorted to snooping and eavesdropping. I became cynical in a veiled attempt to hide my personal fear and confusion. My grades took a dramatic downward curve.

I can't begin to imagine the weight of responsibilities that fell upon my Father during those first weeks. As soon as our school year ended, he asked his sister-in-law to take my brother and me into her home for a few weeks, and we made the move. My aunt had raised three boys and was delighted by another opportunity to mother a small lad. She warmly gave him the loving care he needed so badly at that time. However, she was less than comfortable with me, told me at every opportunity how much she disliked girls and how intensely she wished that I might stay somewhere else. I was overwhelmed with feelings of confusion and rejection. I prayed that I might go home and comforted myself by picturing how happy Father, Brother, and I could be, if we were back home together with me keeping house for us all. My obstinate heart was set on proving that I could handle the small and common tasks of family life and keep things running smoothly, because I wanted desperately to escape the obvious rejection of my aunt.

Father was so preoccupied that I had no opportunity to present my sure solution or to speak of my humiliating rejection. I tried to bear the smarts my aunt inflicted without complaint and comforted myself with assurances that I could take on Mother's role. But Father was making other arrangements that brought an abrupt end to my imaginings. Near the end of summer, he wrote me a letter explaining his plans to send me away to a girls' boarding school. When I read his words that day, I thought my whole world had collapsed. I felt betrayed and abandoned. Although I was thirteen years old, *"I spoke as a child, I understood as a child, I thought as a child"* (1 Cor. 13:11). Eventually I put away childish things, but forty years would pass before I came to understand my Father's wise and loving provision for my true needs.

The bewilderment and anger I continued to experience blossomed into utter despair as I began the fall semester in boarding school. The ninth grade dormitory had no room for me so I was put with the tenth graders where the older girls clearly resented me. My preoccupation with myself left no room for thoughts of God, but He was using all these events to soften my "indocile" heart and make me mistrust my own plans and scheming. If only I had known then that the Master's work in my life would eventually bring an end to my homeless wandering. With utmost patience and marvelous kindness, He was using these small and common things to draw me to Himself.

3. Safely Home

By loneliness, by weary loss of zest;
The rags, the husks, the swine, the hunger-quest,
Drive home the wanderer to the Father's breast! —GMD

In what way does the Master shape individual circumstances to draw His creature back home from the path of destruction? In all of the common circumstances of life, He is molding and shaping; He allows nothing to go to waste. He permits wandering and uses loneliness as a means of drawing us to Himself. Abraham was called to get out of his country and his father's house, to go to an unknown land that God would give his descendants as an inheritance. Joseph was betrayed, separated from his family, and taken as a slave to Egypt where he became God's man to save many from famine. Moses abandoned his position in Egypt, fled to Midian, and spent forty years tending sheep on the backside of the desert before God revealed His plan to redeem His people from bondage. This pattern of forced separation from family appears repeatedly in the biblical record, and we see God's mercy as He uses loneliness and weariness, as means of drawing the wanderer to Himself.

God isolated me, as He did Abraham, Joseph, and Moses, but the result was far different. I chose to wallow in my perverted notion of suffering, deliberately courting loneliness, which was punctuated by the rationing of goods vital to the WWII war effort. Many items were in short supply as assembly lines were converted to produce the machinery of war. American families adapted quickly. Mothers learned to substitute dairy products and fruits for the meat, sugar, and butter that were strictly rationed. Steel and rubber were in such short supply that men had no choice but to learn to repair automobiles and household appliances in order to keep them running. Gasoline allocation followed strict government regulations. I learned early that coin and currency did not guarantee purchasing power; ration coupons represented the gold of the realm. During the months I lived in a dormitory my ration coupons belonged to school officials. Even though I did not need to worry, many of my dreams during those war years were filled with scenes of lost, stolen, or burned up ration coupons. These concerns were unfounded and they added anxiety to the pain I was already nurturing. God allowed my misery to move me, ultimately, closer to Himself.

School rules permitted boarding students to leave campus with a family member for a few hours on Sunday afternoons. In theory, a privilege available to all students, but gasoline was rationed on the basis of the family breadwinner's type of employment. Our family had an "A" coupon which entitled us to only four gallons of gas per week. Father used public transportation all week so that he would have the precious gasoline needed to visit Mother. I could not bring myself to ask him to make a choice, so I feigned the role of a serious student and turned down those weekly opportunities to escape my books. This remarkable "sacrifice" only served to heighten the romantic notion of suffering and isolation that I was experiencing.

Those days of loneliness produced bitterness as I thought about my brother being at home with Father for his school year. They were together; I felt shut out and alone. I grew more preoccupied with Mother's forced confinement and convinced myself that I was surely doomed to follow in her footsteps. I was digging myself into another ditch. My unrealistic response to life's circumstances had progressed from homesickness and loneliness, anxiety and bitterness, to this terrible false perception that I would end up in a mental institution. Anxiety drained away any concern I may have had for good grades. With careless abandon, I threw myself into subdued and subtle rebellion, which further isolated me from schoolmates and darkened my reputation in the dormitory and in the classroom.

I thought that I was creating my own safe place, deep down inside, where I could retreat and enjoy my personal pain. I did not know, then, that God had arranged my isolation, allowed my loneliness, and permitted my wandering. My smoldering rebellion was about to erupt when God provided an English teacher who forced me to consider eternity. She was flamboyant and effervescent, loved drama, and displayed a passion for poetry. Sometimes, in their immaturity, the girls mocked her antics. Personally, her passion thrilled me and prepared my soul for God's truth.

One stormy afternoon, she announced that we would begin a study of "The Hound of Heaven" by Francis Thompson.[1] Never shall I forget the thrill and the fear that seized me with the beginning lines of this truly amazing work. This poem was not about Mr. Thompson; it was about me. I was the one! All that I had ever thought or done was there in this poem. I was running from God, and He was after me. Frightened, but determined, I resolved to run faster. After a lengthy study of "The Hound of Heaven," we were required to memorize the thirteenth chapter of First Corinthians. God was in hot pursuit of my prodigal soul, forcing me to confront my own wickedness.

While I struggled over these issues, Mother was granted a trial period at home and I seized the opportunity to accomplish my own agenda. While running from God, I determined to run right out of the dormitory. I rushed to the office of the Director, and managed, through exaggeration, to persuade him that my mother needed me at home. Through outright deception, I secured his permission to change my status from boarding student to day student. I called the Greyhound bus lines to verify the scheduled morning and evening routes between home and school, and the daily fare. Then I went to work on my parents, convincing them of my new status as a day student. To my amazement they accepted my story. I moved home, and refused to acknowledge that my presence only added to the stress both my parents were experiencing. My desire to get out of the dormitory was temporarily satisfied, but the sense of being hounded by God still weighed on my mind when I decided to attend a week-long series of evangelistic meetings at a local church.

The itinerant preacher's message of salvation did not touch my soul for I had closed my heart to all that was holy. An accomplished chalk artist, he drew frightful pictures of future judgement and, with the help of an eerie black light, stirred up my fears. By the end of the week, his words and pictures convinced me that I was in imminent danger of hell fire. I had no understanding of Christ's sacrifice or of my foul sin that had taken Him to the cross; I heard only the part of the message that I wanted to hear. Fully convinced of God's ability to take me to heaven as a reward for asking, I asked, and I left that meeting mentally persuaded that I was saved and need not fear death. I presumed upon the grace of God, thinking I had been born again, had heaven in my pocket, and now could do whatever I wanted. But God knew my need, loved me, and maintained His pursuit.

Trapped, unknowingly, in that "far country" of deceit, manipulation and self-indulgence, I claimed to be a Christian, a believer in the Lord Jesus Christ, saved, and assured of eternal life. The truth is, I was utterly deceived about God, about His Son, about heaven, and about His eternal plan of salvation. Instead of the peace and joy I expected, failure dogged my every effort, and frustration became my constant companion. Unknown to me, the Master was at work in the midst of my misery and my "weary loss of zest." He was still in pursuit of my soul.

Months rolled into years. Marriage, homemaking, and mother-hood did not fulfill my expectations, and I faced more frequent and intense rounds of frustration as God continued lovingly to pursue me. I tried to clean and polish up my character and to serve God in ways of my own choosing. All such effort on my part was destined for failure because, *"all our righteousnesses are like filthy rags"* (Isa. 64:6). At this stage of my life however, I did not understand that false pretensions of decency and moral stature are contemptible in God's sight. Washing and outward adorning cannot change a pig's love for mud and mire, and neither does a false profession of faith produce righteousness or holy living. Instead, it created in me a great hunger. When the prodigal in the pigpen *"came to himself,"* he saw immediately the foolishness of starving, while back home abundance prevailed. But I was still running from God and deceived about spiritual realities, not willing to admit anything.

Safely Home

God used my rags and husks of self-effort, and my abominable pig-headedness to force me to acknowledge that I was starving, needy, and without spiritual reality in my life. This "hunger-quest" continued to fuel my determination to be free of interference from God, and so my search took the form of a fixed and deliberate plan to read and disqualify the Bible, and to prove to myself that it had no authority over my life. I was really looking for excuses not answers when I initiated my plan to read through the Bible. Ten years had passed since my supposed deliverance from hell, and my decision had not influenced my character or my behaviour.

In disbelief and disdain, I began with Genesis reading methodically through the histories and wisdom literature. Repeatedly, I encountered wanderers: God's own people wandering away from Him, choosing their own way, doing as they pleased. The nation of Israel forgot the miracles God worked on her behalf in bringing His people out of bondage in Egypt. They scorned God's goodness and murmured about His provision for their needs, stirring His anger and bringing judgement upon themselves. As a result, He caused them to wander in the wilderness for forty years before they were permitted to enter the Promised Land (Num. 32:13).

I continued reading, moving from history to poetry, and then to prophecy. I investigated the circumstances of Isaiah's prophetic message to Judah, written seven hundred years before the birth of Jesus Christ. In the fortieth chapter, Isaiah confronted me with the majesty of God. I had no doubts about God as the Creator, and I did not doubt that I would go to heaven. I did not believe much else, but the Master was at work drawing my heart away from the rags and husks, directing this prodigal to look homeward. A. W. Tozer calls this work the "prevenient grace of God, that is, that mysterious, secret working of God in the souls of man, turning them to Himself and mysteriously attracting them to Himself."[2] As I read, God used Isaiah's bold declaration of His majesty to turn my soul toward Himself. I continued reading and in verse twenty-one, I read these questions:

The Master's Work

"Have you not known?
Have you not heard?
Has it not been told you from the beginning?
Have you not understood from the foundation of the earth?"

I hurried quickly over these rhetorical questions that I did not choose to answer and rushed headlong into the next verse: *"It is He that sitteth upon the circle of the earth..."* I reeled, as if struck by lightening! My mind began racing:

Isaiah lived about seven hundred years before Christ was born! Everyone living at that time thought the earth was flat! How could Isaiah have known that the earth was round? He lived more than two thousand years before Columbus! And for all those centuries people had said the earth was flat! Except Isaiah! How did he know? Who told him? Only the Creator could have known! So, God must actually have talked face to face with Isaiah and told him what to write!

God's truth immediately captured my mind. My agenda changed. I desperately wanted to prove the validity of Scripture because I knew that God would tell me, from this book, what I needed to know. Suddenly, every word I was reading became more important than any other I had ever encountered. I began eagerly to read with a different objective. Now I was truly searching, hungry for the truth and open to God's instruction.

I read through the rest of the prophets and into the New Testament searching for God's word to me. In a very short time, I began to comprehend my guilt, to believe that Jesus Christ had paid the penalty for my sin, and to understand why I could trust Him to be both my Saviour and my Lord. Alone, by the side of my bed, I knelt, and in faith, confessed every sin I could recall, and God, the faithful and just One, forgave my sins and washed away all my unrighteousness (1 John 1:9). Relief flooded my soul as I thought of that faithful Sunday school teacher whom God had put in my life so long before. I knew that I had the same forgiveness and peace that she possessed. My tortured wandering behind me, I had come home to the Father's breast. What joy! What rejoicing! God was now my Father and I, the child of His love.

In ways past telling, the Master had woven the small and common events of my life into one tear-stained piece, using them to drive this wanderer home. I testify with the Apostle Paul that, *"He has delivered* [me] *from the power of darkness and translated* [me] *into the kingdom of the Son of His love, in whom* [I] *have redemption through His blood, the forgiveness of sins"* (Col. 1:13, 14). Marvel of marvels, God delivered me from the deception of a false salvation, and made me a child of the King.

I plead with you to examine the ground of your salvation. You dare not remain under the illusion that you are safe for eternity if you have not confessed and repented of your sin. Jesus Christ is the long-promised Messiah. Have you acknowledged Him as your Savior and Redeemer? Reader, take heed to yourself, *"it is appointed for men to die once, but after this the judgment. Nor is there salvation in any other, for there is no other name under heaven given among men by which we must be saved"* (Heb. 9:27; Acts 4:12). Give up your perilous wandering and come home to the Father. Do it now!

4. Divine Purpose

> Too eager I must not be to understand.
> How should the work the Master goes about
> Fit the vague sketch my compasses have planned?
>
> —GMD

To be "too eager" in the context of MacDonald's poem is to be impatient with God concerning spiritual growth and understanding. Our impatience for spiritual maturity can be compared to Abraham and Sarah's impatience for the child God had promised them. Wearied by the long wait, Sarah contrived to bring about the birth through a surrogate mother, thus complicating the lives of Abraham, Isaac, Jacob, and, ultimately, all of their descendants. Generations later, Paul, reflecting on this same immature eagerness, describes the Israelites as having a zeal for God, but not according to knowledge (Rom. 10:2). Young believers often exhibit this misplaced desire. We can have a passionate desire to exercise our faith, but zeal that is not shaped by a mature understanding of Scripture can lead us to make some very bad choices.

MacDonald described my own desire to rush to full maturity when he wrote: "Too eager I must not be to understand." I wanted to be able to understand everything: all the language of Scripture, the spiritual vocabulary of Christian writers, and how God wanted me to live, and, I wanted all these right now. But spiritual growth is not that simple or that swift. In his book, *What Angels Wish They Knew,* Alistair Begg describes this common dilemma, saying:

> The story is told of a street urchin who was taken from his urban setting to the country for the first time. Seeing a songbird on the branch of a tree, he commented, "Poor little bird, he has no cage to live in." His understanding was governed by the life he

knew, and that limited understanding caused him to make mistakes in his assessment of life outside of his environment.[1]

Like the child in the story, I could not even begin to understand divine purpose in freedom.

My understanding of the Christian experience was misinformed by my own personal life history. The physical injuries my brother sustained when he was hit by the car had healed completely, while my impatience with myself erupted more and more frequently in out-bursts of anger. The rejection I experienced in my teen years only increased my anger with those who did not understand me, and with myself, because I could not make them understand. I was in bondage to unattainable goals, not understanding that the chains of my past were broken the moment I confessed my need for forgiveness and put my faith in Christ Jesus as Saviour. He had made me free! But I did not understand all that these truths meant.

I marveled that God was my Father. Awe, wonder, appreciation, new love, and fresh desire fueled my enthusiasm. Eager to study books of the Bible, I wanted to find out all the Word of God had to say about certain subjects and personalities and their life stories.

In my zealous impatience to understand, I kept meeting up with failure. My personal life was clearly a contradiction to the holiness God demands of His children. The heroes of the faith seemed to me, at times, to be as weak and as great a failure as myself. I saw failure as a shameful thing to be avoided. Author, A. B. Simpson describes failure as a building block to spiritual maturity:

> Like his people afterwards and like many a Christian life, Moses had to fail before he could finally succeed. Every true life has a grave behind it, when in lowly and painful crucifixion the strength and confidence of nature were exchanged for the strength of God.[2]

I wanted that exchange in my life. But I was impatient! I wanted to experience the strength of God in the midst of my failure. I did not understand the strongholds of self-reliance, false expectations, and unholy alliances that were still ruling within my heart. Nor could I foresee the countless exchanges that would be necessary to transform my impatience to eagerness for God's purpose rather than my own. Struggling is essential to spiritual growth, but while we are struggling with issues we do not understand, we can do no better than to follow the example of Dora Greenwell, who chose to simply rest in the One she knew as her Saviour:

> I am not skilled to understand
> What God hath willed, what God hath planned;
> I only know at His right hand
> Stands One who is my Saviour.[3]

Knowing the Person of my Saviour is the essence of what salvation means, and is especially important when I am frustrated with my experiences and the ways in which God is saying to me, "wait."

Writers of Scripture tell us that spiritual understanding must be sought with the heart, through meditating on the Word of God, and by prayer. Solomon asked for an understanding heart, and God answered: *"I have given you a wise and understanding heart, so that there has not been anyone like you before you, nor shall any like you arise after you"* (1 Ki. 3:12). Solomon's wisdom remains unparalleled, yet his advice to us seems surprisingly uncomplicated:

> *"Trust in the Lord with all your heart,*
> *And lean not on your own understanding;*
> *In all your ways acknowledge Him,*
> *And He shall direct your paths"* (Prov. 3:5, 6).

Solomon, the wisest of the wise, dared not rely on his own wisdom and understanding. I must follow his example and trust God for the direction I need, waiting for His timing.

The apostle Paul wrote to the Corinthian church, *"I will also pray with the understanding... I will also sing with the understanding"* (1 Cor. 14:15). To the Colossian church he wrote that he would pray for them to *"be filled with the knowledge of His will in all wisdom and spiritual understanding"* (Col. 1:9). To young Timothy he said: *"May the Lord give you understanding in all things"* (2 Tim. 2:7). Paul's letters were written to prevent misunderstandings. In chapters ten and eleven of Romans, he provides a lengthy explanation of the unique saving work the Master accomplished in both Israel and the Gentiles and His gracious provision of mercy. As he concludes the passage, Paul is overwhelmed by the immeasurable, incomparable, infinite wisdom of God, and interrupts himself to exclaim, *"Oh, the depth of the riches both of the wisdom and knowledge of God! How unsearchable are His judgments and His ways past finding out!"* (Rom. 11:33). Without controversy, God's doings are inscrutable and beyond comprehension.

MacDonald is correct: "Too eager I must not be to understand." This unfathomable unfolding of God's wisdom must take place in God's perfect timing. The poet continues with a caution to young believers: "How should the work the Master goes about / Fit the vague sketch my compasses have planned?" The question has to be rhetorical because the eternal plan of the omnipotent God of the universe cannot possibly be contracted to the limits of my understanding.

MacDonald's use of the word "compasses" is appropriate. "A drawing compass is an instrument with two pointed legs connected by a pivot; used for drawing arcs or circles to establish a boundary line or circumference."[4] When I attempt to construct my own circles of understanding, then I tend to think like the urban child in our earlier story, who assumed, because of his limited understanding, that life is best lived in a cage. Not so! God's compass has no boundary line but His great love. I need to allow Him to draw the circles for me because His divine purpose is to set us free: *"Therefore if the Son makes you free, you shall be free indeed"* (John 8:36). And Paul declares: *"Stand fast therefore in the liberty by which Christ has made us free, and do not be entangled again with a yoke of bondage"* (Gal. 5:1). Freed from our own constricted circles of understanding, by the liberating work of our Lord Jesus Christ, our energy may be directed to learning more of the One who is our Master. Our textbook for growth in understanding must be His eternal and unchanging Word, and our time frame also must be what He Himself has prescribed for us.

God intended His dealings with the children of Israel to be written down as a permanent record. After delivering His people from the oppressive Egyptians, the Lord said to Moses, *"Write this for a memorial in the book and recount it... Write these words, for according to the tenor of these words I have made a covenant with you and with Israel"* (Ex. 17:14; 34:27). *"Heaven and earth will pass away,"* Jesus said to His disciples, *"but My words will by no means pass away"* (Matt. 24:35). Jesus' words are written, John tells us, that we might believe that He is the Christ and have eternal life (John 20:31). *"For whatever things were written before were written for our learning, that we through the patience and comfort of the Scriptures might have hope"* (Rom. 15:4). The Lord Himself affirmed to John, on the Isle of Patmos, the permanence of the words of "this book" (Rev. 22:18). Everything God wants us to know, to understand, and to obey, is written in His Word, the only reliable source of truth, and we are to meditate in it day and night.

Spiritual enlightenment and growth in my life come primarily from reading the Bible, but my Master also works through the prose and poetry of fellow travelers. Shortly after my new birth, I learned of the five missionaries who had been killed in a jungle in Ecuador by Auca Indians. In my ignorance, I presumed that misguided zeal had led these Christians to a premature death. I was so wrong. God used Elisabeth Elliot's books, *Through Gates of Splendor, Under the Shadow of The Almighty,* and *The Savage My Kinsman,* to reveal some of the ways He accomplishes His purposes in the lives of His children when they are yielded to His will. So confident, and at peace, were these five men in their obedience to God's clear direction that they did not look for understanding. They were not careless; they were simply obedient to the God they loved without reservation.

From Ecuador, the Master directed my attention to China. I met Isobel Kuhn in her deeply moving autobiographies. In *By Searching*[5] she unfolds the very private and personal details of God's faithful provision for her as she learned to trust Him when both the purse and the bank account were empty, as He prepared her for China. Mrs. Kuhn describes many occasions in *In the Arena*, when she was made a spectacle among the Lisu tribal people with whom she lived. They saw her grappling with the same struggles they faced and witnessed the victory that comes only through Jesus Christ. "The purpose of the arena experience," she writes, "is not for our punishment; it is that God might be revealed."[6] His faithfulness and great power were evident to many in Lisuland who turned to the light of Christ during the years before the Communists invaded China in 1951. Through these powerful missionary accounts I began to see how the Master's work proceeds. God enables us to understand His will, but it is obedience to that will that produces spiritual maturity in our Christian life.

The next tool the Master used in my training program was *The Sunday School Times*, a weekly newspaper published from 1859 to 1965. This strong biblical resource had a profound effect on my early spiritual development, taking me beyond my limited circles of reference into God's wide compass. Stimulating editorials, biblical analysis of world and national news, careful book reviews, and worshipful poetry all spurred my growth as I waited eagerly for each issue to arrive. I am deeply indebted to the publisher for the insight and clear guidance the *Times* provided, and still grieve its untimely demise.

In the beginning of my spiritual growth, my eagerness to understand divine purpose was primarily intellectual. The missionary biographies and the weekly news update emphasized God's desire for both the heathen to hear the gospel, and His faithfulness to be acknowledged. I understood these things in an academic way, but my heart was little involved and my Master would not allow this divide in my soul to remain. He

Divine Purpose

began to surprise me in unlikely places, bringing across my path influences designed to unite my intellect with my heart and will. One of these was a list of Elisabeth Elliot's favorite books and authors, offered on the radio. I kept my dog-eared copy for many years, returning periodically to sample another of her favorites. Looking back over five decades, I marvel at the way God used her suggestions to alter both my mind and my heart.

My first discovery: Amy Carmichael, a British missionary who began a work of rescuing children in India. Some of her rich meditations have been preserved in *Thou Givest... They Gather*. Amy's lesson from Psalm 119:7, 8, became God's instruction to me:

> There was a time when I had to prepare a dear child for a great trial. I knew, though she did not, all that was involved, and everything in me was bent on preparing her to stand strong. Every verse I taught her, every chorus I wrote for her, was bent that way. I learned then more of the heart of God than I had ever known before. Through the love—watchful, constant, and set on strengthening and enabling—that He had given to me, He taught me something of the ways of His love.... The thing that matters is that we should be sensitive to His touch, even though, like the child I taught, we do not in the least know what He is doing. Looking back over these many years, I see the hard rock and the flint-stone turned to standing water, clear pools, springing wells, fountains of water.... Nothing can draw us closer to our Father than these intimate, tender touches of His love.

The lesson: Be sensitive to His love even when, like Amy Carmichael, I do not know what He is doing.

Although I read many of Mrs. Elliot's suggested books, twenty-five years were to pass before I yielded to the wisdom of Francois Fenelon. This seventeenth century churchman wrote letters to certain women in the court of Louis XIV, emphasizing two themes: forget self, love God.[8] From Fenelon I learned the treasures of silence and how to deliberately search out blessings in the midst of life's most trying and noisome situations. Most authors have a few favorite words they use repeatedly. Fenelon loved the word "recollect" and it appears repeatedly in his exceedingly wise instructions for holy living. To recollect is similar to the word meditate. My method: at daybreak, to retrace my steps in order to re-collect all the ways God has guided since yester-morn. I want nothing of value to be lost. These precious re-collections are best preserved in a journal. A simple lined notepad will do. The important thing is to recognize the need to record our dealings with the Almighty in order that we may remember His goodness and give thanks. After Jesus fed the five thousand and the multitude was filled, He said to His disciples, *"Gather up the fragments that remain, so that nothing is lost"* (John 6:12). We do this gathering when we re-collect each day's evidences of grace and mercy. A written record of daily encounters with God helps to clarify our vision. We begin to see how isolated incidents fit into the larger picture of our life. We must never attempt to hurry along this process. Instead, we must patiently wait for the Master to reveal His divine purpose.

There were more books and more years before I made my third important discovery in Elisabeth Elliot's recommended reading list. The English-woman, Lilias Trotter, turned her back on a promising career in art and went to Algeria, where for forty years she devoted her efforts to winning souls for Christ. As a result of her indefatigable work we have the organization now known as Arab World Ministries. Her legacy consists of out-of-print books, leaflets, and sketchbooks, all housed in the Trotter Archives in Loughborough, England. Miss Trotter's writings resonate with the exaltation of her Saviour and reveal a deep personal humility. In *Parables of the Cross*, she explains:

> The Christian life is a process of deliverance out of one world into another, and "death," as has been truly said, "is the only way out of any world in which we are." ... It is in the stages of a plant's growth, it's

budding and blossoming and seed-bearing, that this lesson has come to me: the lesson of death in its delivering power."[9]

In this small but powerful book, Trotter unfolds four critical areas of life where death must be applied: to sin's penalty, to sin itself, to lawful things, and to self. Focusing on a plant's life cycle as her metaphor, she reveals the importance death plays in a life of surrender, justification, holiness, and sacrifice. The word pictures are illustrated with the author's delicate watercolor sketches. She concludes her *Parables* with this appeal to my heart:

> Yes, life is uppermost—resurrection life, radiant and joyful and strong, for we represent down here Him who liveth and was dead and is alive for evermore.... Think of the wonder of it—the Fountain of Life Himself wells up within us, taking the place of all that we have delivered, bit by bit, into His grave. "I live, yet not I, but Christ liveth in me."[10]

Lilias Trotter demonstrated these spiritual truths in the austere way she lived among the Muslims she sought to love into the kingdom of God.

The Master of the universe, the Creator and Sustainer of all things, used a simple list of book recommendations to provide markers on my long road to spiritual maturity. Like the ancient Israelites who set up stones as memorials of times God intervened in their lives, I have books as reminders of His persistent work on my "indocile" heart.

If we continue to abide in Christ, God will continue to reveal more and more of Himself, and we must not impatiently decide how He is going to accomplish this process. We cannot know the ways in which He will surprise us with new glimpses of His heart. But when He intervenes, the revelation will be with undeniable clarity and tenderness. Thus He dealt with lingering doubts from my childhood: why had my father chosen to send me away when all I wanted was to be with him? There had been no answer to my "why?" but the Master's timing is always perfect. One day, as I was reading, forty years of misunderstanding and unresolved issues came into clear focus. The explanation came framed in only thirty-eight words near the beginning of a book of more than 1100 pages. But those few words produced a profound sense of joy and thankfulness in my heart, replacing the self-pity I had so long entertained. Helen Santmyer, in a work of fiction, examines a concerned father's decision to send his daughter away to school after her mother's death. Santmyer explains:

> Her father had wanted Anne out of a house that would be beyond her power to make cheerful. He had probably hoped to preserve her gift of light-heartedness, and so he sent her to board at the...[11]

Smitten with guilt, I recognized the dilemma my own father had faced in the Autumn of 1944, when he was confronted with the question of what to do with me after my mother was institutionalized. He knew that I was far too immature to take on housekeeping duties. My father's desire had been to protect my heart, not to break it. Weeping, I confessed my selfishness and sin, and praised God for His gift of such a wise and caring earthly father. Such is the power of the written word to reveal "how" our Master works His Divine purpose. His work is glorious and marvelous! David expressed his satisfaction this way:

> *"Thou art my hiding place;*
> *Thou shalt preserve me from trouble;*
> *Thou shalt compass me about with songs of deliverance.*
> *Selah."* (Ps. 32:7 KJV).

George MacDonald asks the question: "How should the work the Master goes about fit the vague sketch my compasses have planned?" After a half century of experiencing His work in my life, I understand, with the poet, that the Almighty One cannot, and will not, be confined by my vague notions or

Divine Purpose

expectations. I know His love and provision, apart from merit, His tender nourishing and protection, and I rejoice that, our sufficiency is from God (2 Cor. 3:5). I marvel, and my heart response is Amen and Amen.

5. Ownership Established

I am His house—for Him to go in and out. —GMD

I am His, all His. I am His by creation. I am His by redemption. I have been chosen, adopted, accepted, forgiven. As His child, I have access to wisdom, prudence and a glorious inheritance (Eph. 1:4-11). God had ownership in mind when He sent Moses back to Egypt to present Pharaoh with His demand: *"Let My people go."* Again and again, because Pharaoh refused to recognize God's ownership of the Hebrew nation, the Egyptians suffered through great plagues. Still Pharaoh stood firm against God as Moses announced the tenth judgement: death for every firstborn in Egypt, from the cattle in the stalls to the eldest son in Pharaoh's palace. The children of Israel, trusting God to preserve each of their firstborn, obeyed His instructions to paint the two doorposts and the lintel of their houses with the blood of a lamb. About midnight, the Lord passed through the land of Egypt taking the life of every firstborn living thing, but where He saw the blood, He passed over that house (Ex. 12).

The Hebrews applied the blood of the lamb as instructed, signifying their trust in God. My spiritual house is marked out in like manner. Since the time when I finally trusted God for my personal deliverance, the doorposts and the lintel of my heart have been, and will be, forever identified with the cleansing blood of the Lamb of God, Christ Jesus. I am no longer subject to the death sentence that I was born under. I have been delivered from the kingdom of darkness. God is my Father, and my desire is that my house would be altogether His, for Him to go in and out as He pleases.

The word "house" is used in the Old Testament in a variety of ways. When God said to Abram, *"Get out of your country, from your kindred and from your father's house"* (Gen. 12:1), He was referring to his entire living family, both immediate or extended, all of whom were idol worshipers. When Joshua said, *"But as for me and my house, we will serve the LORD"* (Josh. 24:15), he was referring to the determined response of his own immediate family. When Isaiah visited Hezekiah, who was sick and near death, he said to the king: *"Set your house in order, for you shall die and not live"* (Isa. 38:1). The prophet used the word "house" to refer to both the king's public and private details of life. The word "house" refers to God's holy temple in Psalm 84:10, where the psalmist declared, *"I would rather be a doorkeeper in the house of my God..."* The expression appears again in Psalm 65:4: *"[We] shall be satisfied with the goodness of Your house."* In the Old Testament, the word "house" has multiple applications.

In the New Testament, "house" generally denotes a physical dwelling. The concept of a house church is not new; the early church met in believers' homes where Paul taught from *"house to house"* (Acts 20:20). Paul uses the word "house" to identify the universal body of believers in Ephesians 2:19: *"Now, therefore, you are... fellow citizens with the saints and members of the household of God."* In his epistle to the Corinthians, he refers again to believers using a similar metaphor: *"Do you not know that your body is the temple of the Holy Spirit who is in you, whom you have from God, and you are not your own? For you were bought at a price..."* (1 Cor. 6:19,20). Paul recognized God's ownership, and I need to recognize it too. I am His purchased possession.

The Word of God declares that I am a spiritual house, a holy temple, a dwelling place of God in the Spirit. But, just what does MacDonald mean when he writes, "I am His house—for Him to go in and out"? I find help with this question in the recurring master/servant theme which Jesus develops in several of His parables. (See Appendix, Note B). In the Matthew account, the master comes in, gives an assignment to the servant, then the master goes out; and, after a period of time, he comes in again to evaluate the work done in his absence (Matt. 25:14-30). Inherent in this parable is a solemn warning: the servant must remain faithful in the task entrusted to him, and he must watch continually for the return of the master.

Like the servant in the parable, Christ has committed to me specific obligations that require diligence on my part. And, He said, without reservation: *"He who has My commandments and keeps them, it is he who loves Me. And he who loves Me will be loved by My Father, and I will love him and manifest Myself to him"* (John 14:21). My Master anticipates that I will respond to Him in loving obedience. Then He and His Father will love me and make the divine presence known to me. During these times when I am sensitive to the things of God or when He is teaching me something new and difficult, I am aware of His nearness and presence. When I acknowledge His ownership, the peace of God which surpasses all understanding, guards my heart and my mind, through Christ Jesus (Phil. 4:7). At times I am overwhelmed by His presence. At other times, I don't recognize Him at all. But, whether I am aware or not, I must remember that I am His house, and His house must always be ready for His presence. Is this not what MacDonald means by the lines, "I am His house—for Him to go in and out"?

Sadly, however, I am, like Martha, easily distracted by the concerns of life. Or, like the rich young ruler, I am drawn away by my possessions. Knowing our propensity for self-indulgence, the Author of salvation included in His Word one entire book that depicts the unfolding love story of a mighty king, identified as Solomon, who chooses an immature shepherdess, a Shulamite nobody for his bride. The themes in the Song of Solomon are the same as those woven throughout every redemptive relationship. I see myself, a nobody, without rank or privilege or merit, mysteriously pursued by a loving God, brought into His household, welcomed into His chambers, and invited to participate in the joys of His work.

Song of Solomon begins with the king bringing the Shulamite into his chambers. She hastens to explain that her tanned skin is the result of extended hours working in her brothers' vineyards, to the neglect of her own. Then she asks him this disingenuous question:

> *"Tell me, O you whom I love,*
> *Where you feed your flock?"* (1:7).

There is no hint of chastening in the bridegroom's instructive reply:

> "If you do not know,
> O fairest among women,
> Follow in the footsteps of the flock,
> And feed your little goats
> Beside the shepherds' tents" (1:8).

After some mutual expressions of love, Solomon says to her:

> "Rise up, my love, my fair one,
> And come away" (2:10).

His words are a reminder that there is a time to embrace, and a time to refrain from embracing. Now, other matters require His attention.

The bridegroom seeks the companionship of the bride but she delays, preferring, it seems, to talk of his love rather than share in his work. Patiently, he explains why it is now time for him to go out, and he repeats his request for her to join him:

> "The fig tree puts forth her green figs,
> And the vines with the tender grapes
> Give a good smell.
> Rise up, my love, my fair one,
> And come away!" (2:13).

The king uses exactly the same words he used before, so there can be no misunderstanding his desire for her company. Her reluctance makes us feel uneasy because we see ourselves mirrored in her unseemly response to his repeated invitation. How often do we fail to respond to God's invitation to intimate fellowship?

Ownership Established

The Shulamite chooses to ignore Solomon's request and seeks, instead, to persuade him to stay in with her. Wisely, and tenderly, he teaches her the importance of identifying the destructive tendencies that infect her character:

> *"Catch us the foxes,*
> *The little foxes that spoil the vines,*
> *For our vines have tender grapes"* (2:15).

As keeper of her brothers' vineyards, she understands well the necessity for preventive care of the young vines, for when they are spoiled, the fruitfulness of the entire branch is forever gone. Sin destroys in like manner, but the bride is not willing to recognize her indifference as sinful. She allows her own little sins to creep in and spoil the tender fruit of their love. Ignoring both the invitation and the admonition of her bridegroom, she slips into further self-absorption.

Alexander Maclaren challenges our own complacency as he analyzes the tragic results of self-indulgence:

> All evil, by its very nature, tends to make us insensitive to its presence.... because there are so many things that mask the ebbing away of a Christian life, and because our own self-love and habits come in to hide the declension, let us watch ourselves very narrowly.... So watch, and be sober—sober in our estimate of ourselves, and determined to find every lurking evil, and drag it forth into the light.[1]

If we are to *"catch us the little foxes that spoil the vines,"* we must be serious, watchful, sober, and vigilant, as the apostle has so clearly warned us in 1 Peter 4:7, and 5:8.

Solomon's bride remains self-indulgent and insensitive to the manner of love bestowed upon her. She stays behind, preoccupied with insignificant pursuits. Alone in the night, she finally finds his absence intolerable and expresses her resolve to find him in words that clearly reveal that her attitude has not changed much.

> "I will rise now...
> And go about the city;
> In the streets and in the squares
> I will seek the one I love" (3:2).

The bride speaks of love, but love submits and invests itself in another. What she really seems to be saying is: "I will seek the one I want." She searches for him without success. Then he appears before her, and she takes hold of him tightly.

Like most love stories, all is not well in their relationship. At night, she sleeps while he works. When the bridegroom returns in the night and bids her let him in, she responds selfishly:

> "I have taken off my robe;
> How can I put it on again?
> I have washed my feet;
> How can I defile them?" (5:3).

This careless bride has forgotten to whom she belongs; she is not her own. She lingers long before opening the door only to find him gone from her. J. Hudson Taylor describes the situation with great insight:

> The bride has drifted back from her position of blessing into a state of worldliness. Perhaps the very restfulness of her new found joy made her feel too secure.... Careless of His desire, she thus lightly dismisses Him, with the thought, "A little later I may enjoy His love," and the grieved Bridegroom departs! Poor foolish bride! She will soon find out that the things that once satisfied her can satisfy no

Ownership Established

longer; and that it is easier to turn a deaf ear to His tender call than to recall or find her absent Lord.[2]

Taylor's interpretation is borne out in the text as later in the same chapter, the self-satisfied bride, who would not rise to open the door, becomes dissatisfied, and sets out to look for her absent bridegroom. This second time she goes out into the city at night her experience is far more painful. She says she cannot find him, recruits others to help her search, and gives them a lengthy description of her beloved (5:6-16). Then, to our astonishment, she confesses that she does know where he has gone to work, and how to find him (6:1-3)! Belatedly, she turns to share in his concerns, and experiences the blessing of restored fellowship (6:11; 7:11, 12). The love story concludes with the bride's belated declaration of devotion to her bridegroom. Alas, we often behave like this Shulamite woman: ownership has been established, but we forget that we are not our own.

Precisely because "I am His house—for Him to go in and out," I must ask myself if I too, at times, am guilty of the outright disobedience revealed in the bride's words: *"He knocks, saying, 'Open for me...'"* (5:2). She hears his voice, yet she refuses him his rightful place at her side and will not open the door for him. The Word of God assures me that My Master, Christ Jesus, stands knocking at the door of my heart (Rev. 3:20). Weymouth translates the verse correctly: *"See, I am now standing at the door knocking. If anyone listens to My voice and opens the door, I will come in to him and feast with him, and he shall feast with Me."* When I hear His knock do I deliberately allow self-interest to drown out His words as the king's bride did? What secret sins am I harbouring? What little foxes am I refusing to deal with that are spoiling the vines of intimacy that God would have me enjoy in my love relationship with Him? How have I caused our fellowship to be broken? David offers this insight:

"Who can understand his errors?
Cleanse me from secret faults.

The Master's Work

Keep back Your servant from presumptuous sins;
Let them not have dominion over me" (Ps. 19:12, 13).

As His servant, this should be my constant prayer: no secret or presumptuous sins to spoil fruitfulness. As His bride, there should be no disobedience to quench His love. The door of my heart must be open always for my beloved Master, for I am His house.

In Jesus' parable from Matthew's gospel, we see the servants obedient but careless as to the time of the master's return. In the Song of Solomon, we see the Shulamite available but pre-occupied. Absent in each of these accounts is anticipation, yearning, eager submission, a heart's desire to give pleasure, and a longing for fellowship. If we have not resolved to seek out the little foxes that infest our lives, we too, are in grave danger of unfaithfulness, desertion of duty, and loss of blessing.

Behold my Lord Jesus Christ! He redeemed me at great cost and bestowed His wondrous love upon me. "I am His house -- for Him to go in and out." He is worthy of my total surrender to His love, His purpose, His plans, and His presence. I chose the only rational response to such a Master: to remain forever subject to Him. Marvel of marvels, the Master's high goal for me is to love Him passionately and enjoy the expression of that love by participating in His work. The single-minded obedience for which my soul yearns is perfectly expressed in this prayer by an unnamed Puritan.

> O Lord,
> Let my faith scan every painted bauble,
> and escape every bewitching snare,
> in a victory that overcomes all things....
> I often mourn the absence of my beloved Lord
> whose smile makes earth a paradise,
> whose voice is sweetest music,

Ownership Established

whose presence gives all graces strength.

But by unbelief I often keep Him outside my door.

Let faith give entrance that He may abide with me forever.³

Amen.

6. Under Construction

> He builds me now—and if I cannot see
> At any time what He is doing with me,
> 'Tis that He makes the house for me too grand. —GMD

Those who serve the Master unquestioningly know there will be times when they cannot see what He is doing with them. Noah obeyed God and built the ark even though he had never seen rain. Abraham obeyed God and built an altar for the sacrifice of his only son even though he had never seen anyone raised from the dead. Moses obeyed God and built the tabernacle even though he had never seen such a building used for worship. Noah, Abraham, and Moses cooperated with God in grand building projects that far exceeded their own limited vision. The ark that Noah built, Abraham's altar of sacrifice, and Moses' tabernacle for worship represent fundamental elements of our faith. In ways these men could never have envisioned, God demonstrated His power to save alive from waters of judgement; to provide a substitute sacrifice; and to define the holy character of worship. These three men represent a vast number of faith-filled believers who looked to God for a compass that exceeded all they could ask or think.

Like Noah, Abraham, and Moses, who trusted God for direction, King David relinquished his grand idea of building a cedar house as a dwelling place for God on earth when he heard the Lord's instructions: *"You shall not build a house for My name, because you have been a man of war and have shed blood. Now, it is your son Solomon who shall build My house and My courts, for I have chosen him to be My son, and I will be his Father"* (1 Chr. 28:3, 6). God's "no" to David was loud and clear.

Although prohibited from building the temple, God permitted David a role in making preparations, and the king spent the last years of his life gathering materials for the building. One writer determined the king's personal contribution as 112 tons of gold and 262 tons of refined silver. David also collected: *"bronze and iron beyond measure... hewers and workers of stone and timber, and all types of skillful men for every kind of work"* (1 Chr. 22:14, 15). Even though David could not see clearly what God was doing with him, he affirmed his confidence in the Almighty. Hear his charge to Solomon, given in Jerusalem before all Israel: *"Consider now, for the LORD has chosen you to build a house for the sanctuary; be strong, and do it.... Be strong and of good courage, and do it; do not fear nor be dismayed, for the LORD God—my God—will be with you. He will not leave you nor forsake you, until you have finished all the work for the service of the house of the LORD"* (1 Chr. 28:10, 20). David emphasized not the temple, but the Lord: the Lord's choice of Solomon, the Lord's direction and provision for the work of building, and the Lord's presence from start to finish.

David's resolve to keep his heart fixed on God enabled him to give up his cherished dream. When he heard God's words, "You cannot do that; you can do this," he let go of his ownership of the temple project, and with great energy began assembling the building materials. At his death, Solomon became king, and though the dream had been his father's, Solomon willingly accepted the challenge to build the house for the Lord.

When we cannot see clearly what God is doing in our lives, perhaps we need to let go of something that is not rightly ours. Let us learn from David the blessing that comes when we relinquish expectations and focus our energy on what God **is** allowing us to do. If we are handed someone else's dream, let us seek God's compass with a willing heart and without preconceived limitations. The Master may be testing our level of obedience as part of the building process.

Solomon took on the temple project with enthusiasm. He raised a work force of more than one hundred and eighty thousand men and began construction that took seven years, building the house of God in Jerusalem precisely as shown in the plans his father had received from God. The Scripture says, *"Thus all the work that King Solomon had done for the house of the LORD was finished; and Solomon brought in the things which his father David had dedicated... then the priests brought in the ark of the covenant of the* LORD *to its place... the glory of the* LORD *filled the house of the* LORD" (1 Kings 7:51; 8:6, 11). Thus David's son achieved his father's desire for the Lord's house, making it *"exceedingly magnificent, famous and glorious throughout all countries"* (1 Chr. 22:5). And throughout all history, that unique building has been referred to as Solomon's Temple. The king could not know that God would use his intimate involvement in the temple project to construct a far more important and lasting testimony to the glory of the Lord.

When one reads Chapters five, six, and seven of 1 Kings, and chapters two, three, and four of 2 Chronicles, we see Solomon, not as a kingly overseer but as a major part of the action, observing all that went into the hewing of timbers and stone, and learning firsthand how they needed to be prepared to fit together perfectly. From the information that he gained through his unusual involvement in the construction, he recognized the unique spiritual application and brought that understanding into his writings in the book of Proverbs. Solomon's submission to God in accepting this building program, prepared him, in unique ways, to make a far more significant and enduring spiritual contribution through his writings, than he ever did in the building of the temple. Isaiah declared the eternal character of Scripture superior to the temporary character of building when he said: *"the word of our God stands forever"* (Isa. 40:8). God taught Solomon, through his active involvement in the temple building process, what he needed to understand in order to write his portion of the "wisdom literature" in the Scriptures.

In the first nine chapters of the book of Proverbs, Solomon warns against all manner of evil enticements and invites his readers to make wisdom the true companion of the soul. The king's significant experiences in building the temple are reflected in one grand metaphor:

> *"Wisdom has built her house,*
> *She has hewn out her seven pillars"* (Prov. 9:1).

Although he does not specifically name wisdom's seven pillars, Solomon clearly identifies these characteristics that must undergird each life before one can stand strong and immovable for God. The first pillar of wisdom is the high and holy privilege of giving and receiving fatherly counsel. Ideally, this sonship constitutes an intimate interchange, a building up, between a father/instructor figure, who consistently imparts wisdom, and a son/student who eagerly applies his heart to learn. This pillar of sonship, seen throughout the Word of God, provides the essential prerequisite for the establishment of one's personal house of wisdom.

The other six pillars are interrelated and dependent upon the first. Instruction furnishes training that includes correction designed to effect change. Understanding demonstrates prudence which is quick of apprehension and provides remedy for the simple. Knowledge exhibits discretion concerning that which is right. Enlightenment demonstrates spiritual insight, with purity as the objective. The Fear of the Lord indicates appropriate reverence and awe. Righteousness produces acts of justice, judgement, and equity (See Appendix, Note C).

These seven pillars support Solomon's house of wisdom. Two other passages of Scripture deal with this same concept. In Psalm 19:7-9, David writes:

> "The law of the Lord is perfect, converting the soul;
> The testimony of the Lord is sure, making wise the simple;
> The statutes of the Lord are right, rejoicing the heart;
> The commandment of the Lord is pure, enlightening the eyes;
> The fear of the Lord is clean, enduring forever;
> The judgments of the Lord are true and righteous altogether."

I believe that Solomon learned these eternal truths from his father, and expanded their application as a result of experience gained while building the temple. I think it reasonable also, to believe that Paul deliberately echoed both David and Solomon in Ephesians 1:17, 18, in his prayer for wisdom for all believers: *"That the God of our Lord Jesus Christ, the Father of glory, may give to you the spirit of wisdom and revelation in the knowledge of Him, the eyes of your understanding being enlightened..."* (See Appendix, Note D). James offers further instruction: *"If any of you lacks wisdom, let him ask of God"* (James 1:5). Since all wisdom originates with Him, we should expect to find the same words used to describe wisdom in various portions of Scripture.

Solomon uses the word "hewn" to describe the seven pillars wisdom builds into her house. These principles of spiritual wisdom differ radically from those we would devise for self-improvement, and God's hewing is often accomplished through pain, and at great cost to the individual. The writer of Hebrews makes this very clear: *"Now no chastening seems to be joyful for the present, but grievous; nevertheless, afterward it yields the peaceable fruit of righteousness to those who have been trained by it"* (Heb. 12:11). Isaiah also uses the word "hewn" to encourage Israel to obedience:

> *"Listen to Me, you who follow after righteousness,*
> You who seek the LORD:
> Look to the rock from which you were hewn"* (Isa. 51:1).

The word "hewn" describes something shaped or cut with an ax, knife, or chisel. Like the hewn timbers and hewn stone in Solomon's temple, hewing drastically alters a person or object for the accomplishment of a specific purpose. We find a similar metaphor in the New Testament regarding the way God builds in the life of a believer. Paul called us God's building... the temple of God (1 Cor. 3:9, 16), and His temple is holy and the Spirit of God dwells in it. Scripture frequently employs the building metaphor, and MacDonald acknowledges this repetition when he writes, "He builds me now." Yes. The Holy Spirit dwells in my body. Jesus Christ is the foundation of my faith, *"For no other foundation can anyone lay than that which is laid, which is Jesus Christ"* (1 Cor 3:11). As foretold in Isaiah, Christ is also the measuring line and the plummet, providing Himself as the standard of perfection against which I am being measured (Isa. 28:17). God has appointed salvation for the walls and bulwarks of my temple, and wisdom has hewn out the pillars: sonship, instruction, understanding, knowledge, enlightenment, the fear of the Lord, and righteousness. The Holy Spirit does the work of constructing and fortifying these pillars. He reveals the will of God, strengthens me with power, and enlightens me to comprehend the love of God that surpasses knowledge. He knows what I need in my life. I feel the ax when the Holy Spirit begins to hew down a treasured sin of mine. I feel the knife when He begins to excise murmuring and evil desires. And I experience the chisel daily as the Spirit persists in altering the contours of my character, for I am His living stone and am being built up a spiritual house (1 Pet. 2:5).

Yes, the Master's work continues, and over my head flies a banner: "Under Construction." Since I cannot see what He is doing with me, I need the helpful spotlight provided in the second chapter of Ephesians. Paul's instruction in these verses makes abundantly clear that what was dead is now made alive (1 and 5), that I am raised up (6), given grace and the gift of God (7 and 8), declared to be His workmanship (10), granted peace (14), and made a new creation (15). I am reconciled to God (16) and welcomed as a member of His household (19). A great project is underway as God continues His transforming work.

David did not understand all that God was doing when he was told to assemble the building materials. Solomon did not understand when he was building the temple, the ways in which God was going to use that building as a metaphor so that he could help us understand the seven pillars of wisdom. And centuries later, some of those who witnessed Jesus' miracles of healing could not understand the omnipotent power displayed in the Master's work.

In John's account of the healing of the blind man, the disciples asked their question inside an incredibly small compass. "Who sinned, this man or his parents that caused this man to be born blind?" Jesus exposed their narrow vision with His divine explanation of God's holy purpose: *"Neither this man nor his parents sinned, but that the works of God should be revealed in him"* (John 9:3). Although severely limited in understanding, the man born blind knew a great change had taken place, and he did not flinch before the religious authorities: *"One thing I know: that though I was blind, now I see"* (John 9:25). Should we suppose that God will not use our difficulties to the same end if our sincere desire is to bring glory to His name? And so when our health fails or we are disappointed in love or someone destroys a trust, we can move outside the immediate issue, and recognize that the Almighty Builder is hewing away at our souls to make us into a building that is magnificent.

God is hewing me through the loss of vision associated with Age-Related Macular Degeneration, a disease that now plagues millions of Americans. The onset of AMD brings with it much uncertainty as familiar activities and favorite hobbies must be relinquished. Now I find even the simplest of sewing projects difficult. I have no need for watercolor paints and brushes, and success in reading depends upon lighting and magnification. I am grateful for past opportunities to study perspective in two dimensional art and find those principles a great help as I am faced with confusing visual problems at every turn. While there are many things I can no longer do, I now have time for writing and keeping in touch with precious friends whom I regard as a gift of God. My ministry has taken a quieter, more subdued form, and Bible study is now a consuming passion. Because my eyesight is compromised, my spiritual vision has achieved new dimensions.

The Master is building, building, building; and, when you and I cannot see what He is doing, we can find renewed wonder and hope in Paul's assurance to the Corinthian believers: *"Eye has not seen, nor ear heard, nor have entered into the heart of man the things which God has prepared for those who love Him"* (1 Cor. 2:9). "Since there will be no adversity in Heaven," writes my friend, Daniel Smith, "we commit ourselves to trust God and to obey Him through adversity in this life. Our tears then become special lenses through which we see God in His unfailing love and His determined purpose to remake us into the likeness of

Christ."[1] Our tears enable us to see glimpses of God's compass, for His loving hand has drawn the outline and contour of our every difficulty.

We can see the Master's unfailing love and determined purpose in the life of the man born blind. If the man had not been born that way, we could not look at the glory of God as it was revealed in that man's life. In his tract, "The 'If' in Your Life," A. B. Simpson writes:

> Lord, if thou hadst been here, my brother had not died, and He could have been there; He was not far away. He knew all about it, and He let him die. I think it was very hard for that woman. I have come to think that there is an "if" in every life. It is something that God could have made different, if He had chosen, because He has all power; and yet He has allowed that "if" to be there. I do not discount the "if" in your life. No matter what it is… Come to the Lord with your "if," and let Him say to you what He said to Martha. He met her "if" with His "if"! Said I not unto thee that IF thou wouldest believe, thou shouldest see the glory of God? The glory of God is to come out of the "if" in your life…. [2]

If the man had not been born blind… If the women had not waited to see where they laid the Christ… If Paul's thorn in the flesh had been removed… If God had kept my vision intact… In each of these instances, as in hundreds of others, what blessing would God's people have missed if circumstances had been otherwise. If things had been altered, even a very little, there would be no reason for us to "marvel," but,

> "*He has done marvelous things;…*
> *The* L<small>ORD</small> *has made known His salvation*" (Ps. 98:1,2).

"If I cannot see at any time what He is doing with me, 'tis that He makes the house for me too grand," observes George

MacDonald, and I am grateful for his insight. Even when physical sight is diminished, God removes the scales from spiritual eyes and expands one's ability to recognize that it is in this narrow valley through which He leads that goodness and mercy follow, now, and throughout all the days of our life (Ps. 23:6). I ask myself, am I prepared to follow where He leads? Am I eager for my Master to reveal His divine plan for my life? Am I abandoned to His will? Am I abiding? These are pressing questions as I consider this "too grand" house that God builds for me.

For the fainthearted, or lazy, or those who simply do not understand the holy calling of God, Alexander Maclaren provides both a mild rebuke and a stirring challenge:

> The misery of men is that they pursue aims so narrow and so shabby that they can be attained.... But to have before us an aim which is absolutely unreachable, instead of being, as ignorant people say, an occasion of despair and idleness, is, on the contrary, the very salt of life. It keeps us young, it makes hope immortal, it emancipates from lower pursuits, it diminishes the weight of sorrows, it administers an anesthetic to every pain. If you want to keep life fresh, seek for that which you can never fully find.[3]

The truth is, God calls us to a life of holy and high nobility if we will cooperate with His grace. We can reject His offer, refuse to live within those compasses He has set around us, and live a life of meager destitution. But it need not be that way. Listen! The Master calls. Eagerly, like John the beloved, running to verify for himself the reports of an empty tomb, may we respond to the call of God to follow closely and to yield to the work of the Master who makes this, our house, far "too grand."

7. Grace and Glory

> The house is not for me—it is for Him. —GMD

The Master Builder and the Carpenter of Nazareth are one and the same. He builds me now, in the same persistent, purposeful way that He worked on my indocile heart in small and mysterious ways, ultimately drawing me to Himself. He is building me into a grand house, but "the house is not for me—it is for Him."

God has used this metaphor of building in a variety of contexts. He used it in reference to the universe, *"For every house is built by someone, but He who built all things is God"* (Heb. 3: 4). He used it concerning the nation Israel, *"Unless the LORD builds the house, They labour in vain who build it"* (Ps. 127:1), and He testified beforehand the building work of the Redeemer, saying, *"You shall call your walls Salvation, and your gates Praise"* (Isa. 60:18). The Master Builder established Himself as the foundation, the cornerstone, and the walls of the house He is building.

> *"This was the LORD's doing;*
> *It is marvelous in our eyes"* (Ps. 118:23).

God continues, in the New Testament, to use the building metaphor to show His children their responsibility as part of the house that God is making up of individual believers. The Master's building plan for this house specifically states, *"having been built on the foundation of the apostles and prophets, Jesus Christ Himself being the chief cornerstone, in whom the whole building, being joined together, grows into a holy temple in the Lord, in whom you also are being built together for a habitation of God in the Spirit"* (Eph. 2:20-22). The Lord, with a plumb line in His hand, structured, framed, and named the walls and bulwarks of this house Salvation. "The house is not for me—it is for Him," and He requires my participation in this work.

In Paul's first letter to the Corinthian believers, he informs his readers that they are each a holy temple of God (3:16, 17). This truth is not an isolated statement but an integral part of Chapter Three which outlines clear principles of temple building. Verses 9 and 10 inform us that we are indeed God's building, and, therefore, must exercise deliberate care in how we build on the foundation already laid, which is Jesus Christ. Wisdom is required in selecting suitable building materials (11, 12), for these will be tested by fire and only those which endure will be rewarded (13, 14). Worldly wisdom is futile, of no value in this project because foolishness will perish with this age (18-20). But as to the future, Paul assures us that *"all things are yours, and you are Christ's, and Christ is God's"* (22, 23). Indeed, we are God's building.

The contribution I bring to God's building is like none other. This building is the Master's work, and He calls me to participate wholeheartedly in the construction process. I obey, compelled by love for Him and an intense longing to do His will. He instructs me to build upon His foundation with gold, silver, and precious stones (1 Cor. 3:12), in order that my work will endure when tested by fire. The precious things I bring to this building project are unique. They are my personal works of obedience. I build with Him, *"To the praise of the glory of His grace, and, the word of His grace, is able to build* [me] *up"*(Eph. 1:6; Acts 20:32). God's grace in building, the same grace by which He welcomed me into His family, transforms my acts of obedience into gold, silver and precious stones.

"The house is not for me — it is for Him," and He furnishes the grace needed for the structure to grow. His grace provides the effective working of His power. His grace helps me to understand the unsearchable riches of Christ. His grace gives me access to His manifold wisdom. His grace enables me to comprehend the eternal purpose which He accomplished in Christ Jesus our Lord (Eph. 3:7-11). All, all is of grace, *"That in the ages to come He might show the exceeding riches of His grace in*

His kindness toward us in Christ Jesus" (Eph. 2:7). In a coming day, we shall be set forth as the evidence of His grace, and somehow, display His power, riches, wisdom, and eternal plan to angels. These are His purposes for every believer.

The Word of God speaks much of God's grace which is both rich and sufficient. Actually, His grace is more than sufficient, for *"God is able to make all grace abound toward you, that you, always having all sufficiency in all things, may have an abundance for every good work"* (2 Cor. 9:8). God in Christ Jesus always offers grace, grace always sufficient, grace continually abounding. *"For it is good that the heart be established by grace"* (Heb. 13:9).

In Solomon's temple, gold, silver and precious stones were building materials that could be weighed, measured, and recorded, as we read in a variety of places in the Old Testament record. (See Appendix, Note E). Not so in our temple project. The Master's grace uses building blocks of suffering or affliction to work for us a "weight of glory" that cannot be measured or weighed (2 Cor 4:17). The glory of this treasure belongs to the eternal realm, and we have neither the capacity nor wisdom to determine its true worth.

Paul speaks to us as sons of God, *"and if a son, then an heir of God through Christ"* (Gal. 4:7). In his letter to the Romans, Paul goes further in stating that we are *"joint heirs with Christ, if indeed we suffer with Him, that we may also be glorified together. For... the sufferings of this present time are not worthy to be compared with the glory which shall be revealed in us"* (8:17, 18). To be an heir is to be legally entitled to an inheritance. To be a "joint heir in Christ" means that, by God's grace, we are joined together with Him, we eagerly take on His yoke, we commit to abide in Him, and willingly share in His suffering (Matt. 11:29; John 15:4, 10; Phil. 3:10). By the grace of God, the Author of our salvation was made perfect by the suffering of death, that He might bring many to share His glory (Heb. 2:9, 10). God's grace transforms suffering into glory, and we have the privilege of choosing and participating in God's grace work. Glory, however, is more difficult to define than grace. John, the beloved apostle, gives this testimony, *"And the Word became flesh and dwelt among us, and we beheld His glory, the glory as of the only begotten of the Father, full of grace and truth"* (John 1:14). Grace, therefore, is a presage of glory.

Alexander Maclaren suggests that we err exceedingly when we limit "grace" to a so-called present period of blessedness, and "glory" to a future expectation of what is to unfold in the heavenly realm. He writes:

> Grace and glory are one in essence.... What we have here is a spark which shall be fanned yonder into a radiant flame. But the difference is one of degree, and not of kind. "Grace" is "glory" in the bud; "glory" is "grace" in the fruit.[1]

The apostle Paul expresses this difference, not in kind, but in degree, in several of his letters. To the Romans, he declares that it is Christ Jesus *"through whom also we have access by faith into this grace in which we stand, and rejoice in hope of the glory of God"* (Rom. 5:2). Through faith in Christ, we are given grace to enable us to stand fast and rejoice in present grace, which will yet flower into glory. To the Corinthian believers, Paul writes of the transforming power of grace: *"But we all, with unveiled face, beholding as in a mirror the glory of the Lord, are being transformed into the same image from glory to glory, just as by the Spirit of the Lord"* (2 Cor. 3:18). Through the Holy Spirit, we see the glory of the Lord and are thus transformed into His image. To the Galatians, Paul is vehement: *"God forbid that I should glory except in the cross of our Lord Jesus Christ"* (Gal. 6:14). The central act of history, the cross of Christ, is both grotesque and glorious. The preeminent place of suffering has been transformed, by God's grace, into an exalted place of unspeakable glory. And Peter prays that He will do the same work in us: *"May the God of all grace, who called us to His eternal glory by Christ Jesus, after you have suffered awhile, perfect, establish, strengthen, and settle you"* (1 Pet. 5:10).

Poets and hymn writers have produced a wealth of material focused on glory and thereby have added much to our understanding of this concept. Thomas Blacklock's poem, "Come, O My Soul," contains these two verses that inspire devotion and expectation:

Grace and Glory

> Enthroned amid the radiant spheres,
> He glory like a garment wears;
> To form a robe of light divine,
> Ten thousand suns around Him shine.
>
> In all our Maker's grand design,
> Omnipotence, with wisdom, shines;
> His works, through all this wondrous frame,
> Declare the glory of His Name.[2]

Envision with me God wearing glory like a garment, and meditate upon His works of creation for they declare His unchanging glory.

> *"For the* LORD *God is a sun and shield;*
> *The* LORD *will give grace and glory;*
> *No good thing will He withhold*
> *From those who walk uprightly"* (Ps. 84:11).

On the eve of His departure, the Lord Jesus Christ, in that upper chamber, prayed that we might behold the glory given to Him by His righteous Father (John 17:24), as soon we shall.

One of my favorite poems, "In Immanuel's Land"[3] by Anne R. Cousin, is reported by A. W. Tozer to have nineteen verses, each one itself a song of praise for the glorious abode which is to be our eternal home. Most familiar to many Christians are the verses that appear in hymnbooks with the title, "The Sands of Time Are Sinking" (See Appendix, Note F). The poet writes of the blessed dwelling place promised to every believer, and elaborates on glory: glory because the Dayspring is at hand; glory because His mercy is expansive as the ocean; glory because a poor vile sinner is welcomed into His house of wine; and the glory of the Bridegroom's face and His pierced hand. In

Immanuel's land the Lamb is all the glory! Here, and now, we give God glory when we acknowledge that the excellence of the power is of Him, through Him, and to Him.

God is glorified when we minister to one another with the ability which God supplies, *"that in all things God may be glorified through Jesus Christ, to whom belong the glory and the dominion forever and ever. Amen."* (1 Pet.4:11). How do we do this in practical ways? God's Word is clear: we minister to one another when we equip, encourage, edify, esteem, and exemplify godly behaviour. Scripture abounds with instruction as to how we should relate to one another. Let us look at just a few examples in Paul's letter to the the Ephesians. We equip when we bear with one another in love (4:2), and speak the truth in love (4:15). We minister when we encourage one another to grow up in all things (4:15). We edify one another when we use our mouths for singing, making melody, and giving thanks to the Lord (5:19, 20). A husband and wife esteem one another when he loves her as himself, and she respects him (5:33). And we minister by example when we put on the armour of God and pray for all the saints (6:11, 18).

God, the Master Builder, requires that we *"walk worthy of the calling with which we were called"* (4:1). "The house is not for me — it is for Him," He is worthy, and all glory belongs to Him. Hear the solemn warning of His prophet:

> *"But let him who glories glory in this,*
> *That he understands and knows Me"* (Jer. 9:24).

Abraham, the friend of God, understood and knew God. As a result, *"He did not waver at the promise of God through unbelief, but was strengthened in faith, giving glory to God, and being fully convinced that what He had promised He was also able to perform"* (Rom. 4:20, 21). Therefore, I am resolved to imitate Abraham: to stand unwavering at the promises of my God, to demonstrate faith and obedience in every area of my life, thereby, giving glory to God.

Grace and Glory

There is a note of triumph in MacDonald's words, "The house is not for me -- it is for Him." I agree and offer praise and worship as I present my petition with the Puritan writer:

> O God, Thou God of glory:
> Break me, then bind me up;
> Thus will my heart be a prepared dwelling for my God;
> Then can the Father take up His abode in me,
> Then can the blessed Jesus come with healing in His touch,
> Then can the Holy Spirit descend in sanctifying grace;
> O Holy Trinity, three Persons and one God, inhabit me, a temple consecrated to Thy glory.[4]

Amen.

8. Sovereignty

His royal thoughts require many a stair... —GMD

To kings and potentates belong kingdoms, dominion, and all things royal. George MacDonald distinguishes God's thoughts as "royal," a word used in relation to sovereignty. We read in Scripture of "royal majesty," "royal decrees," and "royal law." Each noun, described by the word "royal," indicates the superior authority of the originator. All of God's thoughts are royal; they proceed from sovereign majesty, many of them pointing to the coming King, *"for God Has highly exalted Him and given Him the name which is above every name, that at the name of Jesus every knee should bow... and that every tongue should confess that Jesus Christ is Lord, to the glory of God the Father"* (Phil. 2:9-11). Christ Jesus is the King of kings. By His life, He disclosed the royal thoughts of His Father, and by His death and resurrection, He secured for Himself the inalienable right to rule and reign as Lord of lords.

> *"Blessing and honour and glory and power*
> *Be to Him who sits on the throne,*
> *And to the Lamb, forever and ever!"* (Rev. 5:13).

To Him belong the kingdom and the royal throne.

From the first word of Genesis to the last word of Revelation, we behold God's unfolding eternal plan. *"In the beginning,"* He spoke creation into existence and declared it all "good," in order that we might know His thoughts and His assessment of His work. Centuries later, He provided ongoing affirmation of His creative power through the prophet Isaiah:

> *"I have declared the former things from the beginning;*

The Master's Work

> *They went forth from My mouth, and I caused them to hear it.*
> *Suddenly I did them, and they came to pass"* (Isa. 48:3).

God, the self-existent, all-powerful, all-wise, ever-present King eternal, immortal, invisible, is Sovereign, yet He chose to reveal to His creation the unchanging process by which He works: He declares; He waits, He acts. His pleasure in His own creative work "in the beginning," is reinforced by these questions and statements:

> *"Lift up your eyes on high,*
> *And see who has created these things....*
> *Have you not known?*
> *Have you not heard?*
> *The everlasting God, the* LORD,
> *The Creator of the ends of the earth,*
> *Neither faints nor is weary"* (Isa. 40:26, 28).

God's sovereignty is emphasized repeatedly by Isaiah.

> *"For thus says the High and Lofty One*
> *Who inhabits eternity, whose name is Holy:*
> *'I dwell in the high and holy place,*
> *With him who has a contrite and humble spirit'"* (Isa. 57:15).

> *"Heaven is My throne,*
> *And earth is My footstool"* (Isa. 66:1).

> *"Remember the former things of old,*
> *For I am God, and there is no other;*
> *I am God, and there is none like Me,*

Sovereignty

Declaring the end from the beginning,
And from ancient times things that are not yet done,
Saying, 'My counsel shall stand,
And I will do all My pleasure'" (Isa. 46:9, 10).

Think of it! The triune God, who is infinitely wise, perfectly satisfied, and eternally fulfilled, created everything for His pleasure! Why? Because love demands an object, and love desires communion with that object. Our God invites us to share His dwelling place and His pleasure forever.

God shared His thoughts with Adam in the garden (Gen. 2:16-18), and with Enoch and Noah as they walked with Him (Gen. 5:24; 6:9). He disclosed His thoughts to Abraham, Isaac and Jacob, with whom He entered into covenant relationship. In the garden, Adam heard God's voice as a question (Gen. 3:9). In the mouth of a cave, Elijah heard God's voice as a whisper (1 Kings 19:9, 12), but to Job His voice sounded like thunder (Job 40:9). David, too, heard that thunder and responded with praise:

"*The God of glory thunders; ...*
The voice of the LORD *is powerful;*
The voice of the LORD *is full of majesty*" (Ps. 29:3, 4).

"*God has spoken once,*
Twice I have heard this:
That power belongs to God" (Ps. 62:11).

Although many Old Testament saints heard God's voice, there were periods of time, some lengthy, when God chose to remain silent—a silence, so far as we know, devoid of visions, messengers, seers, prophets and revelations, a time, it seemed, when the Creator had withdrawn Himself and abandoned His creatures. Not so! In Psalm 19, David affirms that for every moment of recorded time man needs only lift his eyes to behold inescapable evidence of the presence of God, and, therefore, a continuing revelation of His thoughts:

> "The heavens <u>declare</u> the glory of God;
> And the firmament <u>shows</u> His handiwork.
> Day unto day <u>utters</u> speech,
> And night unto night <u>reveals</u> knowledge.
> There is no <u>speech</u> nor <u>language</u>
> Where their voice is not heard" (Ps. 19:1-3).

These underlined words indicate some of the particular ways in which God conveys His thoughts. The creation has never ceased to tell forth the glory of the Creator. God wants us to know His thoughts through the evidence He has provided in the world around us. This testimony has never been silent. It continued during the years Israel was in Egypt, and it continued during the four hundred years between the writing of the Old and New Testaments.

God's sovereignty is emphasized in the very ways His thoughts are described. The author of Psalm 92 tells us that God's thoughts are immeasurably deep (v. 5). Isaac Watts agreed and wrote of the Creator:

> His wisdom's vast, and knows no bounds,
> A deep where all our thoughts are drowned.[1]

Our God who Himself strengthened the foundation of the deep (Prov. 8:26), emphasized the vast dimensions of His thoughts saying,

> "For My thoughts are not your thoughts,
> Nor are your ways My ways," says the Lord.

Sovereignty

> *"For as the heavens are higher than the earth,*
> *So are My ways higher than your ways,*
> *And My thoughts than your thoughts"* (Isa. 55:8, 9).

David, who wrote many of his songs to exalt the sovereignty of his King, marveled at the multitude of God's thoughts.

> *"Your thoughts which are toward us*
> *Cannot be recounted to You in order;*
> *If I would declare and speak of them,*
> *They are more than can be numbered"* (Ps. 40:5).

> *"How precious also are Your thoughts to me, O God!*
> *How great is the sum of them!*
> *If I should count them, they would be more in number than the sand"* (Ps. 139:17, 18).

God's thoughts, which are so deep we could never plumb them, and so high we could never think them, are also beyond our capacity to number. Still, God invites us to think His thoughts after Him. He wants us to try! He wants us to know Him, and the glory and nobility of making the attempt. And there is also a wonder in it, for we wouldn't even try if God did not invite us to do so. Paul tells us, *"God willed to make known the riches of His glory"* (Col. 1:27).

Glorious hymns of praise and expressions of adoration abound in the book of Psalms. This worship is only right and proper from the lips of those who claim to know Him. More astonishing, however, are the declarations of His majesty that originate from some very unlikely candidates for grace, whom the Master uses to declare His glory and to acknowledge His sovereign rights. We will look at four examples.

Rahab, the harlot, admitted to the spies from Israel " ...*our hearts melted; neither did there remain any more courage in anyone because of you, for the* LORD *your God, He is God in heaven above and on earth beneath*" (Josh. 2:11). When the Queen of Sheba saw the riches of Solomon, she said, "*Blessed be the* LORD *your God, who delighted in you... He made you king, to do justice and righteousness*"(1 Kings 10:9). The sovereignty of God is revealed by words of faith and praise and wonder, even when they come from the mouths of women as wicked as these.

Cyrus, the pagan king of the Medes and Persians, testified publicly of God's supreme authority: *"All the kingdoms of the earth the* LORD *God of heaven has given me. And He has commanded me to build Him a house at Jerusalem which is in Judah"* (Ezra 1:2). Cyrus did not understand what he was saying. Nor do we at times. Still, God continually invites us to articulate His holiness and righteousness. Rahab, the Queen of Sheba, and Cyrus, were people who had no time for God or His Word, yet we see the amazing condescension of the God of the universe, as He uses them to boldly proclaim His supremacy.

Nebuchadnezzar, the ruthless king of Babylon, was both arrogant and boastful. His stubborn pride cost him dearly. His kingdom was taken from him; instead of a palace, his dwelling was with the beasts; like an ox, his food was the grass of the field. His humiliation continued for seven years. Then his understanding was restored to him. God wonderfully enabled Nebuchadnezzar to express biblical truth as he publicly blessed the Most High with this amazing testimony:

> "*His dominion is an everlasting dominion,*
> *And His kingdom is from generation to generation.*
> *All the inhabitants of the earth are reputed as nothing;*
> *He does according to His will in the army of heaven*
> *And among the inhabitants of the earth.*
> *No one can restrain His hand*
> *Or say to Him, 'What have you done?'*" (Dan. 4:34, 35).

This fallen and restored ruler gave praise and honour to the King of heaven and declared that all His works are truth, and all His ways justice!

God's royal thoughts and sovereign ways are immeasurably higher than our own. David writes,

> "Such knowledge is too wonderful for me,
> It is high, I cannot attain it" (Ps. 139:6).

Nevertheless, in demonstration of indescribable love, God condescends, sometimes, to allow us to say some right things in the midst of our gross misconception. He is glorified, and we marvel.

Although God concealed Christ in the Old Testament, He was laying the groundwork throughout the books of the law and the prophets for the revelation of Messiah Jesus in the New Testament. For example, in the book of Proverbs, we are confronted with a profound question posed centuries before the birth of Jesus Christ:

> "Who has established all the ends of the earth?
> What is His name, and what is His Son's name,
> If you know?" (Prov. 30:4).

The prophetic content of Agur's question carries the impress of sovereignty, as does the inspired answer which was provided centuries later by Simon Peter: *"Lord, to whom shall we go? You have the words of eternal life. Also we have come to believe and know that You are the Christ, the Son of the living God"* (John 6:68, 69). Peter did not understand the words he spoke at that time. He had no visible reason to make that statement apart from God's clear revelation to him. It was not until he saw Jesus Christ transfigured that he recognized the reality of what he had said earlier. Calling himself an "eyewitnesss to His majesty," Peter testifies to the concept of sovereignty, dominion, power and glory (Matt. 17:1-5; 2 Pet. 1:16).

God ultimately, and finally, has revealed His thoughts through His Son Jesus Christ, who is declared to be the image of the invisible God (Col. 1:15). Jesus, the beloved Son, the living Word, explained, *"I and My Father are one.... I have not spoken on My own authority; but the Father who sent Me gave Me a command, what I should say and what I should speak.... The word which you hear is not Mine but the Father's who sent Me"* (John 10:30; 12:49; 14:24). Every radiant, life-giving word of Jesus was an expression of the thoughts of His Father, and that royal majesty was eminently displayed in Christ's answer to Philip, when he asked to be shown the Father: *"Have I been with you so long, and yet you have not known Me, Philip? ... Do you not believe that I am in the Father, and the Father in Me?"* (John 14:9, 10). Jesus, the Son of God, showed Philip the same longsuffering and patience that His Father had extended to His servant Job centuries earlier.

God graciously permitted Job to express his thoughts and confusion in lengthy monologues interrupted by "friends" who presumed to have superior understanding of both Job's difficulty and God's response. Unaware that God had the situation well in hand, Job pleaded for an audience with Him in order that he might debate his case. His false friends continued their pompous proclamations even as Job suffered.

> *"Then the* Lord *answered Job out of the whirlwind, and said: 'Now prepare yourself like a man; I will question you, and you shall answer Me'"* (Job 38:1,3).

God designed the patient, relentless character of those questions to move Job from his self-righteousness into a sincere acknowledgement of His sovereign authority over all things. As Job admitted, "I don't know; I don't know; I don't know;" he realized the foolish things that he had said about God and the false sense he had had of himself. Then he covered his mouth and bowed in repentance before His Maker. In the presence

Sovereignty

of sovereign majesty, abject humility and true worship are inevitable!

God grants to us the same privilege He extended to Job. In what just might be the most amazing statement in Scripture, God has invited us into His presence for a similar debate:

> "'Come now, and let us reason together,'
> Says the LORD,
> 'Though your sins are like scarlet,
> They shall be as white as snow;
> Though they are red like crimson,
> They shall be as wool.'" (Isa. 1:18).

What an amazing combination of God's sovereign, irresistible grace, and man's capacity to know, to understand, and to choose. The awesome Sovereign of the universe, the Creator of the world, my Maker and Redeemer, invites me to reason with Him: to hear His thoughts and to tell Him mine.

What greater honour could the Creator bestow upon His creatures than to enter into dialogue with them? Wonder of wonders, God offers further explanation and then repeats the invitation:

> "I, even I, am the LORD,
> And besides Me there is no saviour.
> I have declared and saved,
> I have proclaimed, ...
> I, even I, am He who blots out your transgressions for My own sake;
> And I will not remember your sins.
> Put Me in remembrance;

The Master's Work

Let us contend together;
State your case, that you may be acquitted" (Isa. 43:11, 12, 25, 26).

We are invited into the presence of the King and told to speak freely. Aware that God has spoken in His holiness (Ps. 108:7), we should respond by falling on our face in prayer, pleading mercy and forgiveness.

As we consider the revelation of God's majesty in the created universe, recollect His words to Abraham, Enoch, Noah, and other Old Testament saints, and examine the testimony of unbelievers and believers alike, we must agree with MacDonald that "His royal thoughts require many a stair," for they are very deep, very high, exceedingly precious, and too numerous to recount. The Lofty One whose name is Holy astonishes us with a further guarantee of His loving provision:

"As His divine power has given to us all things that pertain to life and godliness, through the knowledge of Him… by which have been given to us exceedingly great and precious promises, that through these you may be partakers of the divine nature…" (2 Pet. 1:3, 4).

Amazing! We are invited to come aside and reason with Him. He has assured us of every provision for life and godliness. Our thoughtful response is but the echo of His royal thoughts.

> *"To God our Saviour,*
> *Who alone is wise,*
> *Be glory and majesty,*
> *Dominion and power,*
> *Both now and forever. Amen."* (Jude 25).

9. Precious Promises

>His royal thoughts require many a stair,
>Many a tower, many an outlook fair;
>Of which I have no thought, and need no care. —GMD

God's royal thoughts are expressed as statements for our learning, as commands for our protection, and, as promises, precious promises, that we may live in full assurance of hope. His thoughts are revealed through His compassions "that are new every morning," and through His kindness that is ever "merciful," "marvelous," and "abundant" (Lam. 3:23; Ps. 117:2; 31:21; Neh. 9:17). Thus we are encouraged to know our God.

Jesus Christ spoke His Father's thoughts and all *"marveled at the gracious words which proceeded out of His mouth... For no man ever spoke like this Man!"* (Luke 4:22; John 7:46). He warned us, His followers, not to worry about life: what we will eat, what we will drink, what we will put on. Instead, He directs our attention to the sovereignty of God by giving both a command and a promise: *"Your heavenly Father knows that you need all these things. But seek first the kingdom of God, and His righteousness, and all these things shall be added to you"* (Matt. 6:32, 33). Obedience to this command requires a determined dedication to understand God's royal thoughts regarding His kingdom and His righteousness.

God's holy character and the kingdom that He will one day establish are founded upon the reality of His personal love. The apostle Paul's prayer for the Ephesian believers stresses personal responsibility: *"that you being rooted and grounded in love, may be able to comprehend with all the saints what is the width and length and the depth and height—to know the love of Christ, which passes knowledge"* (Eph. 3:17-19). Paul wants us to pray that the Holy Spirit might reveal to us these God-thoughts as they are manifested in the majestic person of His Son. The apostle pulled the past, present, and future together when he wrote that God has *"made known to us the mystery of His will... that in the dispensation of the fullness of the times He might gather together in one all things in Christ, both which are in heaven and which are on earth"* (Eph. 1:9, 10). This is the loving plan of the High and Lofty One who is *"clothed with majesty"* (Ps. 93:1); *"His name alone is exalted"*(Ps. 148:13). This One is my Master and, in love, He has made known these royal thoughts to all who believe.

In a discussion of this incomparable love of Christ, Alexander Maclaren maintains, "It all comes because this Heaven-descended Christ has come down the long staircase of Incarnation..."[1] MacDonald surely agrees when he writes, "His royal thoughts require many a stair." No matter how earnestly I may wish to know the ways of God, there will be no progress so long as my thoughts and concerns are focused on the things of this world. The Word of God is clear:

"Lift up your eyes to the heavens" (Isa. 51:6).

"Let us lift up our hearts and hands to God in heaven" (Lam. 3:41).

"I lift up my hands toward Your holy sanctuary." (Ps. 28:2)

"To You, O Lord, I lift up my soul" (Ps. 25:1).

All Scripture agrees that I am to lift up my eyes, my heart, my hands, and my soul, as I desire to understand His royal thoughts.

The prophet Amos has much to say about God's determination to communicate with His people. He affirms that God does nothing, unless He reveals His secrets to His servants (3:7). Then Amos calls our attention to His marvels and His name:

*"For behold, He who forms mountains,
And creates the wind,*

Precious Promises

> Who declares to man what his thought is,
> And makes the morning darkness,
> Who treads the high places of the earth —
> The LORD God of hosts is His name" (Amos 4:13).

What a verse! We see God's omnipotence: He forms mountains and creates wind. We see His omniscience: He tells me what I think. We see His omnipresence: He subjects all things to Himself. We hear His name: LORD God of hosts. Wonder of wonders, He deigns to communicate these truths about Himself to me!

> "He who builds His layers in the sky...
> The LORD is His name" (Amos 9:6).

The New King James Bible notes that "stairs" is an equivalent translation of the word "layers." David Levy, author of "Israel The Nation of Destiny," a study of Amos 9, agreed when he wrote that this great God, who controls the universe, built stairs to His throne in the heavens.[2] This spatial metaphor represents both accessibility and the need for ascent. Amos explains in these verses that Almighty God, knowing the thoughts of man, still, chooses to reveal Himself and provides a way of access. MacDonald may very well have had Amos 9:6 in mind when he wrote, "His royal thoughts require many a stair."

MacDonald also draws on David's experience as a warrior, one who clearly understood the military advantage of "many a tower." In the spiritual realm, David acknowledged God as his tower and refuge:

> "Hear my cry, O God;
> Attend to my prayer.
> For You have been a shelter for me,
> And a strong tower from the enemy" (Ps. 61:1,3).

David's plea for personal protection melts into resolve and then becomes confidence in the last verse of the psalm. Knowing that he had a *"strong tower from the enemy"* allowed him to look up with rejoicing and praise.

In our poem, MacDonald moves from the need for stairs and towers to the outlook fair that is requisite to a proper appreciation of the thoughts of God. In the practical realm, our usual and most familiar fair outlook is limited to our view through window glass. Our homes would be a dreary place without windows through which we delight to look upon growing things: stately trees, and blooming flowers. If we lift our eyes heavenward we behold wispy clouds and ethereal blue. Heaven, we are told, has windows, that are like open hatches through which flows God's extravagance. What might Noah have glimpsed as he focused heavenward through that eighteen inch opening at the top of the ark? The biblical account tells us that the "windows of heaven" were opened and water poured out upon the earth (Gen. 7:11). Noah was being preserved in the middle of worldwide judgement; the days and days of rain were fulfillment of what God had said He would do. For Noah, this deluge was a demonstration of divine power and sovereign judgement, an opportunity for his confidence to grow and his hope to increase. Noah's obedience to God's word motivated his first act after leaving the ark: building an altar and offering sacrifice to God. And every time we see a rainbow we are reminded of God's great promise to Noah.

In the last book of the Old Testament, we hear the Lord of hosts declare that the "windows of heaven" will pour out precious promises:

> *"Prove Me now…*
> *If I will not open for you the windows of heaven*
> *And pour out for you such blessing*
> *That there will not be room enough to receive it"* (Mal. 3:10).

The "windows of heaven" testify to God's profusion. Noah saw power and judgement poured forth, and Malachi promised blessing that could not be measured or contained. MacDonald was correct: "His royal thoughts require many a stair, many a tower, many an outlook fair."

As His children, we rejoice in God's blessing and hope, for *"hope does not disappoint, because the love of God has been poured out in our hearts by the Holy Spirit who was given to us..."* (Rom. 5:5). Believing that God has poured out this love on us as an expression of His royal thoughts, we possess, without controversy, an "outlook fair." This outlook transforms everything, enabling us to lift eyes and heart and hands and soul to God so that our lives become one wonderful, continual hymn of praise.

God's royal thoughts, which He wants us to know and believe, He reveals through His Word, which is to be welcomed *"not as the word of men, but as it is in truth, the word of God, which also effectively works in you who believe"* (1 Th. 2:13). Of what value are my insignificant efforts to raise a ladder to heaven or try to create a mountain top experience for myself? These are all of naught, as we are reminded so forcefully by Solomon's admission upon completion of the "magnificent, famous and glorious" temple in Jerusalem: *"Behold, heaven and the heaven of heavens cannot contain You. How much less this temple which I have built!"* (1 Kings 8:27). In the fictional work, *The Laird's Inheritance*, Mr. Simon counsels Cosmo about understanding God: "To truly know, He will have us go in at the great door of obedient faith.... If anyone thinks he has found a back stair into the house of the knowledge of God, he will find it lands him at a doorless wall."[3] MacDonald's words at the head of this chapter are correct: to be free from self-effort and without presumption is to have "an outlook fair; of which I have no thought, and need no care."

God's thoughts are so unlike our own that they are almost one hundred eighty degrees contradictory to what we think. One example of this contradiction is the biblical connection between humility and greatness. Jesus said that the way up is down, and His disciple explains submission this way:

The Master's Work

"*Therefore humble yourselves under the mighty hand of God, that He may exalt you in due time*" (1 Pet. 5:6). God turns everything inside out; so if a believer tries to absorb the fact that the way up is down, without God's power, he certainly will find himself at a doorless wall, unable to make sense out of what seems to be a profound contradiction in terms. The key to understanding God's thoughts, is confessing that we cannot. Then, in great mercy, God will undertake for us.

I am commanded to humble myself, to take an active role in submission, but transformation, by the renewal of my mind, is the work of the Master as I yield to Him. Notice the verbs David uses to define our responsibility:

> "*Trust in the* LORD, *and do good;*
> *...Feed on His faithfulness.*
> *Delight yourself also in the Lord,*
> *And He shall give you the desires of your heart.*
> *Commit your way to the* LORD,
> *Trust also in Him,*
> *And He shall bring it to pass*" (Ps. 37:3-5).

Yes. He will bring spiritual understanding to pass as I trust, feed, delight, and commit. None of these things David counsels me to do will produce spiritual maturity directly, but if I will do these things, then God will give me the spiritual understanding I desire. Why? Because: "*The* LORD *thinks upon me*" (Ps. 40:17). He is the great Initiator. He loves me. He revealed Himself to me in the world that He created, in the prophets that He sent, and ultimately in the person of His Son. We **only** love Him because He first loved us (1 John 4:19). He has made precious promises and continually demonstrates His love as He goes before and prepares the way for me to understand. Unlike human masters, my Master wants me to follow His voice, stay by His side, and keep my eyes on Him, so that I do not miss even a whisper of instruction or direction.

> *"Behold, as the eyes of servants look to the hand of their masters,*
> *As the eyes of a maid to the hand of her mistress,*
> *So our eyes look to the LORD our God,*
> *Until He has mercy on us"* (Ps. 123:2).

And He will have mercy on us for He has promised. The prophet Jeremiah shows clearly the relationship between God's merciful thoughts about us and the "outlook fair" which He provides:

> *"For I know the thoughts that I think toward you, says the LORD,*
> *Thoughts of peace and not of evil, to give you a future and a hope"* (Jer. 29:11).

Jeremiah is enabled to maintain an "outlook fair" because he knows God's thoughts are toward him for his good.

Paul, too, has an outlook fair that is based on God's unchanging Word. He makes this clear when he writes to the Corinthian believers, *"All the promises of God in* [Christ] *are Yes, and in Him Amen, to the glory of God through us"* (2 Cor. 1:20). The apostle challenges us to live on a higher plane in order that God may be glorified in us! And, recognizing that this is God's purpose for my life, not that I would become successful but that God would be glorified in me and through me, provides a rich and transforming "outlook fair."

Peter agrees, and opens before us an outlook that is fairer than fair, when he writes, *"As His divine power has given to us... Exceedingly great and precious promises that through these you may be partakers of the divine nature... For so an entrance will be supplied to you abundantly into the everlasting kingdom of our Lord and Saviour Jesus Christ"* (2 Pet. 1:3, 4, 11). We should not be distracted by reversals in life and our outlook should not be altered by circumstances. We are not victims. We are sons and daughters of the King of kings. He has given us precious promises and He will keep them.

The Master's Work

Our royal outlook rests on God alone. As His servant, I have but one Master and one duty: loving obedience and submission to Him who is pledged to care for me, to sustain me, and to enable me both to obey and to submit. I need have no concern, for my Master never calls me to a task without making provision for all that is needed to accomplish the work. "[He] *is able to do exceedingly abundantly above all that we ask or think*" (Eph. 3:20). To meditate upon these God-thoughts is to fling aside the stupefying limits of our finite understanding and stand agape in wonder and adoration.

This morning I awoke very early as I am wont to do most days. Long years of habit have not dulled for me the delight of being alone with my Lord in the darkness that comes before the dawn. I came to my comfortable, well-lit corner with anticipation, as always, that God and I might meet the day together. After a quiet time of reading, recollection, and prayer, I applied myself to the consideration of "His royal thoughts" toward me.

Overtaken by sleepiness, I removed my glasses, switched off the light, and lay down on the couch for a wee nap. Shortly thereafter, I was awakened by sunlight streaming through the wood slats of the shuttered eastern window. My arm was extended with an upturned hand that appeared to hold a cupful of liquid gold; every line and crease in my palm seemed remodeled. It was not just my hand that appeared transformed; my poor eyes, without benefit of corrective lenses, were able to define the contours with amazing clarity. I stared, entranced, for it seemed that I could see my cup of gold overflowing with His grace and love. Then slowly, very slowly, I extended my fingers and as my hand lay flat in the dazzling sunlight, it appeared to reflect the light, as if a mirror, and I saw the spiritual lesson: when we hold things within our own cupped hand, they are ours alone; only when we extend our hand and let go the golden treasures, can we begin to serve others, to send forth His light, to become, by His grace, a reflection of Himself, that God may be glorified through us.

Relinquishment, then, is the first step to experiencing God's gift to us of an "outlook fair," but it is only the first of many steps. Over and over in the Word of God I see the necessity for surrender, for abandonment, for release, for yielding, for submission. These are the requirements of His cross. Christ Jesus calls me to surrender, *"He who loves his life will lose it, and he who hates his life in this world will keep it for eternal life. If anyone serves Me, let him follow Me; and where I am, there My servant will be also"* (John 12:25, 26). Obeying is yielding. I need have no thought, no care, for what has been relinquished. The Son of God calls me to submission, saying, "I am the way. Follow Me." And He demonstrates for me the extent of the commitment, *"O My Father, if it is possible, let this cup pass from Me; nevertheless, not as I will, but as You will"* (Matt. 26:39). Jesus relinquished all to save my soul. In thankfulness and joy I am to relinquish all for Him.

Paul was very specific when describing his personal experience of abandonment of all for Christ:

> *"What things were gain to me, these I have counted loss for Christ. But indeed I also count all things loss for the excellence of the knowledge of Christ Jesus my Lord, for whom I have suffered the loss of all things, and count them as rubbish, that I may gain Christ and be found in Him, not having my own righteousness, which is from the law, but that which is through faith in Christ, the righteousness which is from God by faith"* (Phil. 3:7-9).

As we obey and submit, God changes our perceptions, and we acquire the "outlook fair" that MacDonald is writing about.

For Paul, there was even more compelling motivation. He was truly determined to have **all** that God had promised when he declared unequivocally: *"That I may know Him and the power of His resurrection, and the fellowship of His sufferings, being conformed to His death... I press on, that I may lay hold of that for which Christ Jesus has also laid hold of me"* (Phil. 3:10, 12). Do we have this kind of resolve?

This house my Master is building is for Himself. Christ Jesus is the foundation; the walls are called Salvation; the upper chambers are His design. He builds the stairs, and the configuration of vaulted arches and high towers provide protection and an outlook fairer than fair, that I, too, *"may know Him and the power of His resurrection."*

> *"Such knowledge is too wonderful for me;*
> *It is high, I cannot attain it"* (Ps. 139:6).

> *"I will meditate on the glorious splendor of Your majesty,*
> *…Your kingdom is an everlasting kingdom,*
> *And Your dominion endures throughout all generations"*
> (Ps. 145:5, 13).

O, Lord God Almighty, as the heavens are higher than the earth, so are Your ways higher than my ways, and Your thoughts than my thoughts. Help me as I meditate on Your glorious majesty to bring every thought into captivity to the obedience of Christ (2 Cor. 10:5). Amen.

10. Omnipotence

> Where I am most perplexed, it may be there
> Thou mak'st a secret chamber, holy-dim,
> Where Thou wilt come to help my deepest prayer.
>
> —GMD

Our poetic journey with George MacDonald began with consideration of the way the Master works in small and common things to draw individuals safely home to Himself, and how He reveals His royal thoughts, and how He demonstrates His sovereignty and omnipotence. He lays the foundation and instructs our building process, Paul informs us, *"that in the ages to come He might show the exceeding riches of His grace in His kindness toward us in Christ Jesus"* (Eph. 2:7). We have Jesus' testimony that this work never ceases: *"My Father has been working until now, and I have been working,"* He assured His disciples (John 5:17). Now, and always, He is changing my life: convicting, redeeming, renewing, transforming and fulfilling His promise that *"the God of all grace, who called* [me] *to His eternal glory by Christ Jesus, will... perfect, establish, strengthen, and settle* [me]*"* (1 Pet. 5:10). His precious promises furnish my "outlook fair" and guarantee my eternal future.

MacDonald turns from a lofty contemplation of God's glorious majesty to a clear acknowledgement of the perplexities that we allow to complicate our lives and cloud our vision. When David's rebellious son Absalom was killed, the king became so distracted by grief that he failed to see how God had preserved his kingdom for him. If I allow distractions to move into my soul, I too, will fail to recognize the hand of God at work in my life. Distractions produce distortions which feed our natural inclination toward fear, anxiety, and perplexity. To our shame, we often forget Paul's simple command, *"Be anxious for nothing"* (Phil. 4:6), which permits no wiggle room.

Jesus warned of a coming time of great distress upon earth: the sea and the waves roaring, the powers of heaven shaken, and men's hearts failing them for fear. In the face of such catastrophes our Master offers a remedy, *"Look up and lift up your heads"* (Luke 21:28). Whether one is faced with great distress or the common needs of the day matters not; the cure for fear is ever the same, reject thoughts of worry or anxiety and replace them with thoughts of trust in a Father who knows the things we need (Luke 12:22, 29, 30). Paul repeats Christ's wise counsel, *"Set your mind on things above, not on things on the earth"* (Col. 3:2). However, we do indeed live on earth, and, as we know all too well, the most tranquil of hours can be shattered when something unexpected occurs. We are so quickly distracted, so prone to fretfulness, and ultimately, to murmuring. In these moments of "perplexity," we would do well to recollect the words of the psalmist:

> *"In the time of trouble*
> *He shall hide me in His pavilion;*
> *In the secret place of His tabernacle"* (Ps. 27:5).

> *"In the multitude of my anxieties within me,*
> *Your comforts delight my soul"* (Ps. 94:19).

Where I am perplexed, there, I must resolve to act in faith, *"casting all* [my] *care upon Him, for He cares for* [me]*"* (1 Pet. 5:7). Where life seems uncertain, there, I am called to obey. I am *"not to be soon shaken in mind or troubled, either by spirit or by word or by letter"* (2 Thes. 2:2), for *"God has not given* [me] *a spirit of fear, but of power and of love and of a sound mind"* (2 Tim. 1:7). Where I am perplexed or fearful, there, there, my Lord draws near and assures me that He is my *"God, in truth and righteousness"* (Zech. 8:8), and so I affirm with David,

Omnipotence

*"I sought the L*ORD*, and He heard me,
And delivered me from all my fears"* (Ps. 34:4).

Wherever I find myself, God is present with me and He is sufficient.

Alexander Maclaren provides a glowing description of this all-sufficiency of Omnipotence:

> "I will be to them" — then in all dark places there will be a light, and in all perplexities there will be a path, and in all anxieties there will be quietness, and in all troubles there will be a hidden light of joy, and in every circumstance life will be saturated with an Almighty Presence which shall make the rough places plain and crooked things straight.[1]

A lovely picture of this all-sufficiency is recorded in the book of First Kings, where we read of a notable woman in Shunem who identified the prophet Elisha as *"a holy man of God."* With her husband's permission, she furnished a small upper chamber, on the wall of her home with a bed, a table, a chair, and a lamp stand, and whenever Elisha passed that way, he turned in there to rest and be refreshed.

The little chamber became a place of blessing to both Elisha and the woman. There, to her great amazement, Elisha prophesied that she would bear a son. When he was still but a lad, the boy died quite suddenly, and there, in that little chamber, she laid his body on the prophet's bed, shut the door, and went out to seek Elisha. There, in the prophet's chamber, she received her dead son raised back to life, and, there she bowed herself in most profound gratitude (2 Kings 4:8-37). The room was only a small, sparsely furnished upper chamber, but there, in that secret corner on a high wall, wondrous, life-changing events took place. Where she was "most perplexed," there the Master wrought His works of grace.

Daniel faced the same kind of perplexity. His life of active service extended through the entire seventy year period of the Babylonian captivity. As a child, while still in Judea, Daniel must have made a personal choice to dedicate himself to God. His remarkable strength of character is revealed, when, as a teenager, *"Daniel purposed in his heart that he would not defile himself with the portion of the king's delicacies"* (Dan. 1:8). This resolve enabled him to resist continuing pressures to conform to the culture of the Babylonian court. His steadfast proclamation of the sovereignty and power of God is recorded in Scripture and continues to resonate to this day. We learn of Daniel's amazing influence with four powerful kings: Nebuchadnezzar, Belshazzar, Cyrus, and Darius. Daniel's most severe test came when a decree was made that anyone who petitioned any god or man other than the king, should be cast into the lions' den. We read:

> *"Now when Daniel knew that the writing was signed, he went home. And in his upper room, with his windows open toward Jerusalem, he knelt down on his knees three times that day, and prayed and gave thanks before his God,* **as was his custom since early days***"* (Dan. 6:10). [Bolding added.]

Daniel allowed nothing to deter him: he purposed in his heart; he prayed, as was his custom; he set his face toward the Lord God as he had done from his youth.

The decree was signed, and, according to the law of the Medes and Persians, it could not be altered. The terms of the document were final. The deadly conspiracy of his enemies was real. The den of lions was frightfully real. But Daniel's response was to do that which had been his custom since early days: he prayed and gave thanks. Daniel was determined, disciplined, dependable. And God protected his life. Following his unforgettable deliverance from the lions' den, he gave this triumphant, concise explanation to King Darius, *"My God sent His angel and shut the lions' mouths"* (Dan. 6:22).

Omnipotence

God may not send an angel nor shut the lions' mouths in answer to your urgent plea for help, but rest assured, if your established custom is to faithfully offer thanksgiving to God and ask for His guidance in every situation, then you may confidently look for His help. A. B. Simpson expressed his unshakeable confidence in God in this way:

> How are Thy servants blessed, O Lord!
> How sure is their defense!
> Eternal wisdom is their guide,
> Their help omnipotence.[2]

God is no respecter of persons. He responded to the need of the unknown, unnamed woman in Shunem with the same kind attention and provision he made for Daniel, a prominent public figure in the most powerful kingdom at that time. God loves and cares for each of us in the same way, without partiality. Such knowledge should cause us to shout our praises. But, even as we revel in the assurance of His great unchanging love, we are faced with potential danger if we unwittingly open the door to presumption, a very real danger, which seems to be little understood in our day. Presumption is taking something or someone for granted; an overstepping of proper boundaries. We must not presume upon God. David acknowledged this ever-present danger, prayed for God's help, and recorded his experience for our learning.

Out of an overflowing heart, David wrote Psalm 19. He begins this exquisite tribute with praise for the enduring testimony of creation (1-6). Next he extols the wisdom of all forms of God's instructions (7-9), and sets their true value far above all manner of earthly riches and palatable delights (10). Following his brief, but all encompassing examination of the heavens and God's purpose for man, the psalmist moves us to the "secret chamber," the "holy-dim" place of communion with God. With the door fast shut to all that would distract or dismay, David agrees with God about His royal instructions,

The Master's Work

> "Moreover by them Your servant is warned,
> And in keeping them there is great reward" (Ps. 19:11).

These words gently remind us that we are servants, God's servants. Our duty is unquestioning obedience, the ground of our hope for reward. But how can we keep God's commands? David asks, *"Who can understand his errors?"* (12). He knew that he could not. I know that I cannot. In sorrow, I acknowledge that my errors are beyond number and I am "most perplexed." Where? There, in the secret place of communion with God. As MacDonald has written, "It may be there Thou mak'st a secret chamber, holy-dim, where Thou wilt come to help my deepest prayer." Here I am, blessed Master. Help me understand my errors; cleanse me from secret faults (12). Protect me when the enemy has ended his attack and I taste the sweet confidence that may follow an hour of righteous living, for there, at that juncture, the danger of presumption is most real. David knew this danger well, and so he prayed,

> "Keep back Your servant also from presumptuous sins;
> Let them not have dominion over me" (v.13).

Eagerly, I acknowledge my position and make his prayer my own: Because I am Your servant, my Father, I can make this petition. I am accepted in Your family, made one of Your children, and know the indescribable joys and delight of Your household. This loving relationship overwhelms me, but I fear that in the bonds of love I may unwittingly overstep or presume. I understand that I have not because I ask not, but I dread that I might ask amiss (James 4:3). Only Your grace, My God, and the power of Your Holy Spirit can keep me from the snare of presumption. Fill me with Your Spirit; guide me, *"keep back Your servant from presumptuous sins,"* I pray.

David expresses confidence that God had accepted his prayer and answered his petition, and he hastens to define the peace that he is experiencing:

> "Then I shall be blameless,
> And I shall be innocent of great transgression" (v.13).

What a marvel this: that we shall be seen blameless and innocent before the omnipotent Sovereign of the universe.

> "But certainly God has heard me;
> He has attended to the voice of my prayer.
> Blessed be God,
> Who has not turned away my prayer,
> Nor His mercy from me!" (Ps. 66:19, 20). Amen.

The apostle John provides further instruction concerning the claiming of God's promises without the danger of presumption: *"Now this is the confidence that we have in Him, that if we ask anything according to His will, He hears us. And if we know that He hears us, whatever we ask, we know that we have the petitions that we have asked of Him"* (1 John 5:14, 15). Both David and John challenge us to consider our perplexities in the light of God's omnipotence.

In the closing chapter of Luke's gospel we see the disbelief and confusion that marred the response of Christ's followers when they did not find the body of the Lord Jesus Christ in the tomb. Luke writes:

> "On the first day of the week, very early in the morning, they... came to the tomb bringing the spices which they had prepared.... Then they went in and did not find the body of the Lord Jesus.... Then they returned from the tomb and told all these things ... to the apostles.... Peter arose and ran to the tomb; and stooping down, he saw the linen cloths lying by themselves; and he departed, marveling to himself at what had happened" (Luke 24:1, 3, 9, 10, 12).

Peter did not marvel because of belief, but because of unbelief. We know from John's account of these events, that *"they did not know the Scripture, that He must rise again from the dead"* (John 20:9). Peter could not understand. He was dismayed at not finding the body. "Most perplexed," Peter and John told no one, and went to their own homes.

We understand how the rock-hewn chamber of death had been sealed with a great stone, but the darkness of the tomb could not hold the Bright and Morning Star (Rev. 22:16). In triumphant majesty, He broke the bonds of death. Christ Jesus came forth from the grave! Luke reports the blazing light of angelic beings shining forth as they announced the triumphant victory of His resurrection: *"He is not here, but is risen!"* (Luke 24:6).

That same morning, Luke tells us, two of His disciples set forth on a seven-mile journey from Jerusalem to Emmaus. They were greatly perplexed by the events that had taken place with regard to Jesus of Nazareth, whom they had hoped was going to redeem Israel. They pondered the reports of certain women who had visited the tomb and had seen a vision of angels saying that He was alive (vv.19-23). Later, these disciples returned to Jerusalem and announced to the others, 'The Lord is risen indeed." As they were speaking, Jesus Himself came and stood in their midst, and they all were terrified. When He showed them His hands and His feet, they did not believe for joy, and they marveled (vv.34-41).

We see great perplexity on the part of the women, Peter and John, the two on the road to Emmaus, the rest of the disciples, and those gathered with them. Nevertheless, back in that holy-dim, rock-hewn chamber the dead body of Christ Jesus had indeed been raised to life. His hands and His feet bore the nail prints. He ate food in their presence, and, He opened their understanding that they might comprehend the Scriptures. Then He explained, "[I]*t was necessary for the Christ to suffer and to rise from the dead the third day"* (vv.45–46). All the perplexities of all the centuries were resolved by the One who said: *"All things must be fulfilled which were written in the law of Moses and the Prophets and the Psalms concerning Me"* (v.44).

In the 24 chapter in Luke, we find the lovely word *"behold."* With respect to the women, Luke writes, *"Behold, two men stood by them in shining garments"* (v.4). He uses the word again to focus upon the two travelers: *"Behold, two of them were traveling that same day to a village called Emmaus"* (v.13). And the risen Lord Jesus uses the word to direct attention to that which identifies His omnipotence: *"Behold My hands and My feet, that it is I myself"* (v.39), and, *"Behold, I send the Promise of My Father upon you"* (v.49). Jesus was careful to have us know that we are not to marvel because we must be born again, nor are we to marvel when the dead hear the voice of the Son of God (John 3:7; 5:28); but we are to marvel because: *"The Father loves the Son, and shows Him all things that He Himself does; and He will show Him greater works than these, that you may marvel"* (John 5:20).

Christ Jesus chides us gently but firmly, saying: *"But you, when you pray, go into your room, and when you have shut your door, pray to your Father who is in the secret place; and your Father who sees in secret will reward you openly"* (Matt. 6:6). Where I am "most perplexed," confused, bewildered, floundering; there, He comes to that secret place to help me pray. There, He comes to me in the fullness of His power, in the stillness of His love, to fill me with His Spirit, and a lowly closet is transformed into a holy trysting place, where my Beloved says, Wait patiently, *"Let the word of Christ dwell in you richly in all wisdom"* (Col. 3:16). Where? There, in that secret chamber. Why? Because I am His. How? By becoming a partaker of Christ (1 Cor. 2:16; Heb. 3:14).

Recently, in the margin of a treasured old Bible, next to the verse that speaks of Abraham's intercession on behalf of righteous persons in the city of Sodom, I found this quotation from T. E. Brown which speaks of the Master's profound help in prayer:

> How entered, by what secret stair I know not,
> Knowing only, He was there.[3]

It is to the small, shut room within, that I retreat for prayer. It is there, hidden within the bloodstained doorposts and lintel of my inner house, in that secret chamber, made holy-dim by the shadow of the Master's out-stretched hand, that He comes

The Master's Work

"to help my deepest prayer." The omnipotent Lord of glory draws near, resolves my perplexities, gifts me with the fullness of His Holy Spirit, and invites me to behold and to marvel, as I watch my Master at His work. In humble submission I worship and affirm:

> Nor Time, nor Place, nor Chance, nor Death can bow
> My least desires unto the least remove;
> He's firmly mine by oath; I His by vow;
> He's mine by faith; and I am His by love;
> He's mine by water; I am His by wine;
> Thus I my best-beloved's am; thus He is mine.[4]

Francis Quarles 1592-1644

Appendix

Chapter 1

Note A. References to the use of the word "tent" as it applies to our natural body appear in Isa. 38:12; 2 Cor. 5:1; and 2 Peter 1:13.

Chapter 5

Note B. The master/servant parables referred to are:
Matt. 25:14-30;
Mark 12:1-9; 13:33-37;
Luke 12:34-40, 42-48; and 17:1-10.

Chapter 6

Note C. Proverbs references for seven pillars of wisdom.

Sonship: 1:8; 2:1; 3:11, 12; 4:1, 10, 20; 5:7; 6:1,3; 7:1; 8:32.

Instruction: 1:8,23; 2:10; 3:1; 4:13; 5:23; 6:23; 7:25; 8:6, 33; 9:9.

Understanding:1:5,22; 2:2,6,11; 3:5,13; 4:1,5,7; 5:1; 7:4; 8:1,5,12,14; 9:4, 6.

Knowledge: 1:4; 2:5, 10; 3:21; 4:23; 5:2; 6:16; 7:1; 8:6, 9; 9:10.

Enlightenment: 2:3; 3:18; 4:21; 6:23; 7:2; 8:10; 9:9.

Fear of God: 1:7, 29; 2:5; 3:7; 8:13; 9:10.

Righteousness: 1:3; 2:9,20; 3:3; 8:18, 20.

This list is not exhaustive.

Note D. Parallel teaching by David, Solomon, and Paul. David identifies scriptural blessing for his son. See Psalm 19.

Law instructs; understanding makes the simple wise; knowledge is right; enlightenment purifies; the fear of the Lord endures; judgement is righteous. Solomon identifies seven pillars of wisdom. Compare Note C above. Paul prayed that his spiritual children might know the riches of their inheritance, thus demonstrating one aspect of sonship. See Eph. 1:17, 18. He lists: wisdom and revelation, knowledge, understanding, and enlightenment.

Chapter 7

Note E. Some Old Testament references to the weight of building materials used in Solomon's temple.

The weight of gold:

Josh. 7:21; 2 Sam. 12:30; 1 Kings 10:14; 1 Chr. 20:2; 21:25.

The weight of silver:

1 Chr. 28:14, 17; Ezra 8:30; Isa. 46:6; Gen. 23:16; Job 28:15.

The weight of stone:

2 Sam. 12:30; 1 Kings 10:2; Prov. 17:8; Eze. 27:22 ; Dan. 11:38.

Note F. "In Immanuel's Land" by Anne R. Cousin, 1824-1906. These five verses generally appear in hymnbooks under the title "The Sands of Time Are Sinking."

> The sands of time are sinking,
> The dawn of Heaven breaks,
> The summer morn I've sighed for,
> The fair sweet morn awakes:
> Dark, dark hath been the midnight,
> But Dayspring is at hand,
> And glory—glory dwelleth
> In Immanuel's land.

Appendix

Oh! Christ He is the Fountain,
The deep sweet well of love!
The streams on earth I've tasted,
More deep I'll drink above:
There, to an ocean fulness,
His mercy doth expand,
And glory—glory dwelleth
In Immanuel's land.

With mercy and with judgement
My web of time He wove,
And aye the dews of sorrow
Were lustered with His love.
I'll bless the hand that guided,
I'll bless the heart that plann'd,
When throned where glory dwelleth
In Immanuel's land.

Oh! I am my Beloved's,
And my Beloved is mine!
He brings a poor vile sinner
Into His "House of wine."
I stand upon His merit,
I know no other stand,
Not e'en where glory dwelleth
In Immanuel's land.

The bride eyes not her garment,
But her dear Bridegroom's face;
I will not gaze at glory,

The Master's Work

But on my King of Grace—
Not at the crown He giveth,
But on His pierced hand:
The Lamb is all the glory
In Immanuel's land.[1]

Notes

Chapter 1 THAT YOU MAY MARVEL
1 Kate Seredy, *The Good Master* (New York: Viking, 1935) 32.
2 George MacDonald, *Diary of An Old Soul* (Minneapolis: Augsburg, 1944) 70-4.
3 MacDonald 72, 74.

Chapter 2 SMALL AND COMMON
1 Charles Wesley, "And Can It Be?" *Hymns for the Family of God* (Nashville:Paragon, 1976) 260.

Chapter 3 SAFELY HOME
1 Francis Thompson, "The Hound of Heaven," *A Treasury of the World's Best Loved Poems* (New York: Avenel, 1961) 166-170.
2 A.W. Tozer, *Christ the Eternal Son* (Camp Hill: Christian Publications, 1991) 143.

Chapter 4 DIVINE PURPOSE
1 Alistair Begg, *What Angels Wish They Knew* (Chicago: Moody, 1998) 196-7.
2 A. B. Simpson, *Seeing the Invisible* (Camp Hill: Christian Publications, 1994) 77.
3 Dora Greenwell, "I Am Not Skilled to Understand," Philip Comfort and Daniel Partner, *The One Year Book of Poetry* (Wheaton: Tyndale, 1999) March 26.
4 *Webster's New World College Dictionary* (New York: Macmillan USA, 1999) 297.
5 Isobel Kuhn, *By Searching* (Chicago: Moody, 1959).
6 Isobel Kuhn, *In the Arena* (Chicago: Moody, 1958) 8.

7 Amy Carmichael, *Thou Givest... They Gather* (Fort Washington: Christian Literature Crusade, 1958) 6-7.

8 Francois Fenelon, *Spiritual Letters to Women* (New Canaan: Keats, 1980).

9 Lilias Trotter, *Parables of the Cross* (Upper Darby: Arab World Ministries, n. d.) 1.

10 Trotter 26-7.

11 Helen Hoover *Santmyer,... and ladies of the club* (New York: Putnam's, 1982) 21.

Chapter 5 OWNERSHIP ESTABLISHED

1 Alexander Maclaren, *Music For The Soul* (Chattanooga: AMG, 1996) 322.

2 J. Hudson Taylor, *Union and Communion* (Chicago: Moody, n. d.) 48, 55-6.

3 "Faith and the World," *The Valley of Vision*, ed. Arthur Bennett (Carlisle, PA: Banner of Truth Trust, 1975) 107.

Chapter 6 UNDER CONSTRUCTION

1 Daniel H. Smith, "Divine Optometry," *Emmaus News Bulletin*.

2 A B. Simpson, "The 'If' in Your Life," Isobel Kuhn, *Green Leaf in Drought* (Robsonia, PA: OMF, 1983) 42-3.

3 Maclaren 237.

Chapter 7 GRACE AND GLORY

1 Maclaren 213.

2 Thomas Blacklock, "Come, O My Soul," A. W. Tozer, *The Christian Book of Mystical Verse* (Camp Hill, PA: Christian Publications, 1963) 83.

3 Anne Cousin, "In Immanuel's Land," Tozer, *Mystical* 141.

4 "O Fountain of All Good," Bennett 6.

Notes

Chapter 8 SOVEREIGNTY

1 Isaac Watts quoted by William MacDonald, *Alone in Majesty* (Nashville: Nelson, 1994) 139.

Chapter 9 PRECIOUS PROMISES

1 Maclaren 282.

2 David Levy, "Israel The Nation of Destiny." *Israel My Glory* June/July 1990, 26.

3 George MacDonald, *The Laird's Inheritance* (Minneapolis: Bethany, 1987) 154.

Chapter 10 OMNIPOTENCE

1 Maclaren 163.

2 Simpson, *Seeing* 172.

3 T. E. Brown quoted by Amy Carmichael, 3.

4 Francis Quarles quoted by Warren W. Wiersbe, ed., *Anthology of Jesus* (Grand Rapids: Kregel, 1981) 107.

APPENDIX

1 Anne Cousin, "In Immanuel's Land," Tozer, *Mystical*, 123-7.

Scripture Index

Chapter 1 THAT YOU MAY MARVEL

Job	37:5	12
Psalm	118:22, 23	9
Isaiah	1:2,3	14
	29:14	12
Micah	7:15	12
Habakkuk	1:5	12
Matthew	8:27	9
Mark	5:20	10
Luke	20:22-26	10
John	3:7	11
	5:8,9	11
	5:17	12
	5:19, 20	11
	5:25	11
	5:28, 29	11
	6:29	12
	7:14,15	10
	8:28	10
	8:38	10
	9:4	12
	10:25	12
	12:49, 50	10
	14:26	13
	16:8	13
	17:4	13
1 Corinthians	2:9,10	13

Chapter 2 SMALL AND COMMON

Psalm	7:14, 15	23
	69:7, 8	24
	75:6, 7	20
Acts	8:21	19

113

	13:9	17
1 Corinthians	13:11	26
Ephesians	2:23	21
1 Timothy	1:16	17
2 Peter	3:9	21

Chapter 3 SAFELY HOME

Numbers	32:13	31
Isaiah	40:21, 22	32
	64:6	30
Acts	4:12	33
Colossians	1:13, 14	33
Hebrews	9:27	33
1 John	1:9	32

Chapter 4 DIVINE PURPOSE

Exodus	17:14	39
	34:27	39
1 Kings	3:12	37
Psalm	32:7	42
	119:7, 8	41
	119:18	39
Proverbs	3:5, 6	37
Matthew	24:35	39
John	6:12	42
	8:36	39
	20:31	39
Romans	10:2	35
	11:33	38
	15:4	39
1 Corinthians	14:15	38
2 Corinthians	3:5	45
Galatians	5:1	39
Colossians	1:9	38
2 Timothy	2:7	38
Revelation	22:18	39

Scripture Index

Chapter 5 OWNERSHIP ESTABLISHED

Book	Reference	Page
Genesis	12:1	47
Exodus	12	47
Joshua	24:15	48
Psalm	19:12, 13	54
	65:4	48
	84:10	48
Song of Solomon	1:7	49
	1:8	50
	2:10	50
	2:13	50
	2:15	51
	3:2	52
	5:2	53
	5:3	52
	5:6-16	53
	6:1-3	53
	6:11	53
	7:11, 12	53
Isaiah	38:1	48
Matthew	25:14-30	48
John	14:21	49
Acts	20:20	48
1 Corinthians	6:19, 20	48
Ephesians	1:4-11	47
	2:19	48
Philippians	4:7	49
1 Peter	4:7	51
	5:8	51
Revelation	3:20	53

Chapter 6 UNDER CONSTRUCTION

Book	Reference	Page
1 Kings	5, 6, 7	59
	7:51	59
	8:6, 11	59
1 Chronicles	22:5	59
	22:14, 15	58

	28:3, 6	57
	28:10, 20	58
2 Chronicles	2, 3, 4	59
Psalm	19:7-9	60
	23:6	65
	98:1, 2	64
Proverbs	9:1	59
Isaiah	28:17	62
	40:8	59
	51:1	61
John	9:3	63
	9:25	63
1 Corinthians	2:9	63
	3:9, 16	61
	3:11	61
Ephesians	1:17, 18	61
	2:1-19	62
Hebrews	12:11	61
James	1:5	61
1 Peter	2:5	62

Chapter 7 GRACE AND GLORY

Psalm	84:11	71
	118:23	67
	127:1	67
Isaiah	60:18	67
Jeremiah	9:24	72
Matthew	11:29	69
John	1:14	70
	15:4, 10	69
	17:24	71
Acts	20:32	68
Romans	4:20, 21	72
	5:2	70
	8:17, 18	69
1 Corinthians	3:9-33	68
2 Corinthians	3:18	70
	4:17	69

Scripture Index

	9:8	69
Galatians	4:7	69
	6:14	70
Ephesians	1:6	68
	2:7	69
	2:20-22	67
	3:7-11	68
	4:1	72
	4:2, 15	72
	5:19, 20, 33	72
	6:11, 18	72
Philippians	3:10	69
Hebrews	2:9, 10	69
	3:4	67
	13:9	69
1 Peter	4:11	72
	5:10	70

Chapter 8 SOVEREIGNTY

Genesis	2:16-18	77
	3:9	77
	5:24	77
	6:9	77
Joshua	2:11	80
1 Kings	10:9	80
	19:9, 12	77
Ezra	1:2	80
Job	38:1, 3	82
	40:9	77
Psalm	19:1-3	78
	29:3, 4	77
	40:5	79
	62:11	77
	92:5	78
	108:7	84
	139:6	81
	139:17, 18	79
Proverbs	8:26	78

Isaiah	30:4	81
	1:18	83
	40:26, 28	76
	43:11, 12, 25, 26	84
	46:9, 10	77
	48:3	76
	55:8, 9	79
	57:15	76
	66:1	76
Daniel	4:34, 35	80
Matthew	17:1-5	82
John	6:68, 69	81
	10:30	82
	12:49	82
	14:9, 10	82
	14:24	82
Philippians	2:9-11	75
Colossians	1:27	79
2 Peter	1:3, 4	84
	1:16	82
Jude	25	84
Revelation	5:13	75

Chapter 9 PRECIOUS PROMISES

Genesis	7:11	88
1 Kings	8:27	89
Nehemiah	9:17	85
Psalm	25:1	86
	28:2	86
	31:21	85
	37:3-5	90
	40:17	90
	61:1, 3	87
	93:1	86
	117:2	85
	123:2	91
	139:6	94

Scripture Index

	145:5, 13	94
	148:13	86
Isaiah	51:6	86
Jeremiah	29:11	91
Lamentations	3:23	85
	3:41	86
Amos	3:7	86
	4:13	87
	9:6	87
Malachi	3:10	88
Matthew	6:32, 33	85
	26:39	93
Luke	4:22	85
John	7:46	85
	12:25, 26	93
Romans	5:5	89
2 Corinthians	1:20	91
	10:5	94
Ephesians	1:9, 10	86
	3:17-19	85
	3:20	92
Philippians	3:7-9	93
	3:10-12	93
1 Thessalonians	2:13	89
1 Peter	5:6	90
2 Peter	1:3, 4, 11	91
1 John	4:19	90

Chapter 10 OMNIPOTENCE

2 Kings	4:8-37	97
Psalm	19	99-101
	27:5	96
	34:4	97
	66:19, 20	101
	94:19	96
Daniel	1:8	98
	6:10	98
	6:22	98

Zechariah	8:8	96
Matthew	6:6	103
Luke	12:22, 29, 30	96
	21:28	96
	24:1-49	101-103
John	3:7	103
	5:17	95
	5:20	103
	5:28	103
	20:9	102
1 Corinthians	2:16	103
Ephesians	2:7	95
Philippians	4:6	96
Colossians	3:2	96
	3:16	103
2 Thessalonians	2:2	96
2 Timothy	1:7	96
Hebrews	3:14	103
James	4:3	100
1 Peter	5:7	96
	5:10	95
1 John	5:14, 15	101
Revelation	22:16	102

APPENDIX

Genesis	23:16	106
Joshua	7:21	106
2 Samuel	12:30	(listed twice) 106
1 Kings	10:2	106
	10:14	106
1 Chronicles	20:2; 21:25	106
	28:14, 17	106
Ezra	8:30	106
Job	28:15	106
Psalm	19	10
Proverbs	1-9	105
	17:8	106
Isaiah	38:12	105

Scripture Index

Ezekiel	46:6 106
Daniel	27:22 106
Matthew	11:38 106
Mark	25:14-30 105
	12:1-9 105
	13:33-37 105
Luke	12:34-40, 42-48 . 105
	17:1-10 105
2 Corinthians	5:1 105
Ephesians	1:17, 18 106
2 Peter	1:13 105

O My Soul
A Biblical Exploration of Soul-talk

O My Soul is the first book written by Marilyn. Here is why she wrote this wonderful encouragement: I had struggled for some time to learn to bring my thoughts into captivity to Jesus Christ, as we are admonished in 2 Corinthians 10:5. It became apparent in my study of God's Word that those who managed to so discipline their minds talked, not to themselves, but to their immortal soul. Over a period of four or five years, I collected an astounding list of Bible passages about soul-talk and began to understand that when my soul is blessing God, I cannot be complaining, worrying, or arguing. However, I cannot bless the Lord until I cast down thoughts that exalt themselves against the knowledge of God. After I rebuke those wicked ideas, I can talk to my soul in biblical phrases somewhat like praying the words of Scripture back to God. I felt compelled to share the results of this spiritual journey with others who struggle in their thought life as I have.

CPSIA information can be obtained at www.ICGtesting.com
259844BV00004B/7/P